Praise for *The Spiritual Magic of Dolls*

"Najah Lightfoot's *The Spiritual Magic of Dolls* is an enchanting guide for us magical souls who cherish dolls. Through her captivating personal stories of the dolls from her personal collection, Najah reveals the magic she has made with these cherished little spirits. The words she weaves enlighten, delight and vindicate those of us who know that dolls are so much more than just toys. If you've sensed the magic within your dolls but never fully understood it, Najah becomes your trusted guide, unveiling how dolls can become powerful partners in your spiritual and magical practices." —Madame Pamita, author of *The Witch's Guide to Animal Familiars, Magical Tarot, Baba Yaga's Book of Witchcraft*, and *The Book of Candle Magic*

"If you love dolls or wonder why you're so drawn to them or you're curious about how to work magic with them, this book is for you. Najah is the perfect guide to doll magic—her experience is vast, and her enthusiasm is contagious." —Tess Whitehurst, author of *The Halloween Forever Oracle* and *The Oracle of Daydreams and Moonbeams*

"Najah Lightfoot has gifted us with a beautiful tribute to the magick of dolls and deepened our understanding of their spiritual potential. *The Spiritual Magic of Dolls*, featuring personal anecdotes against a historical backdrop and with elucidating illustrations, is one for all doll lovers to treasure. Lightfoot has composed a classic addition to the magick makers' library." —Priestess Stephanie Rose Bird, author of numerous books including *Sticks, Stones, Roots, and Bones, The Healing Tree,* and *Motherland Herbal*

"With every doll you find, buy, rescue, or gift, let this book be your guide to the enchanted mystery of dolls. As Najah Lightfoot reveals her tender

vulnerability, we reignite our dormant, curious wonder of innocence from when we first shared our secret language with dolls. *The Spiritual Magic of Dolls* reminds us that magic is in everything." —Terry Iacuzzo, author of *Small Mediums at Large*

"As a doll lover, an empath, and a purveyor of strange and wonderful dolls, I found *The Spiritual Magic of Dolls* to be a remarkable, intelligent peek into the world of personal magick, as well as the magick of dolls. I love this book; anyone with a love for magick dolls will love this book, and anyone skeptical of magick should read it too. You will discover how our beloved dolls can become powerful conduits for intuition and spiritual growth. Najah Lightfoot provides expert guidance on integrating dolls into your daily practices, transforming them from mere collectibles into sacred companions on your spiritual path." —Kat Blowers, owner of FugitiveKatCreations, a paranormal doll shop

"*The Spiritual Magic of Dolls* by Najah Lightfoot explores the profound importance of dolls in society. With threads of symbolism and cultural significance, the author evokes the deep connections made each time a doll enters someone's life. This enchanting journey will bring you vivid reminders of every doll you have ever loved." —Laura Louella, coeditor of *Brigid's Light*

"In Najah Lightfoot's book, *The Spiritual Magic of Dolls*, you will discover that dolls are more than just tangible, inanimate objects to be admired on a shelf. Whether cherished heirlooms, forgotten finds, or brand new in the box, Lightfoot guides you into the enchanted world of doll magic. Behind their delicate, painted porcelain faces and lifelike glass eyes, there lies a secret and magical world of doll consciousness. Immersed within this world, Lightfoot lovingly shares how dolls are an integral part of her magical practice. With years of experience and a deep connection to the spiritual realm, Lightfoot brings her unique insights and wisdom to help

you learn to communicate as well as establish a working relationship with these powerful magical allies." —Toni Rotonda, owner of the Buckland Museum of Witchcraft and Magick

"Najah Lightfoot is a master storyteller. *The Spiritual Magic of Dolls* is no exception. Her lifelong relationship with dolls gives her a unique insight into their properties—magical, psychological, and social—and transports the reader into places strange and wonderful. Using a storehouse of wisdom and experience, her dolls create for the reader a bridge between the natural orders of things and the world as we humans experience it." —Jesse Bransford, author of *A Book of Staves*, artist, and clinical professor of art, New York University

"*The Spiritual Magic of Dolls* by Najah Lightfoot is an enchanting exploration of dolls as vessels of magic, memory, and spirit. Through heartfelt personal stories, vivid recollections, and fascinating histories of select dolls, Najah shares how these sacred companions hold space for healing, power, and ancestral connection. Her deep love and reverence for her dollies shines through every chapter and, as I turned the pages, I was gently reminded of a beloved doll from my own childhood. This is a radiant and insightful offering for anyone who delights in the quiet pull of charmed things and the blessings hidden in their stitches." —Cairelle Crow Perilloux, author of *The Magic in Your Genes*

"I am always looking for new explorations of magical objects, and with *The Spiritual Magic of Dolls,* Najah Lightfoot took me along on a great adventure exploring her world of enchanted companions. Within these pages are thrills, chills, and ancient sacred knowledge, all revolving around what many consider just an innocent child's toy." —Steven Intermill, director of the Buckland Museum of Witchcraft and Magick

"Najah Lightfoot's *The Spiritual Magic of Dolls* is a treasure trove of stories. She discusses how to bring a new-to-you doll into your home,

how to find dolls in vintage shops, even how to leave a doll behind—with kindness. From initiating your doll into your magical life to dolls in film, Najah delves into doll lore with an exquisite attention to detail. This book took me back to my own childhood and the dolls my grandmother made for me. I now regret giving away many of those dolls—to family members, but still, I miss them, and even more so after reading Najah's book. I also found a couple of dolls made by my grandmother that were buried in my closet. I brought them out, dusted them off, and placed them where I could incorporate them into my daily life once more. If you love dolls, collect dolls, make dolls, or otherwise make space for dolls in your life, you definitely want this magical book." —Christine Cunningham Ashworth, author of *Scott Cunningham—The Path Taken*

"Fascinating, surprising, and deeply educational, *The Spiritual Magic of Dolls* is a rare book about a very daring—and somewhat secretive—subject. At times eerie, at times dreamlike, these pages come alive with the whispered promise of enchantment. Thankfully, Najah Lightfoot explores the complex and often overlooked history of dolls and then leads readers into the realm of their unique and mind-blowing magic. The result is a book that is at once moving and memorable—a book that has a place on the bookshelf of every magical practitioner and doll enthusiast." —Antonio Pagliarulo, author of *The Evil Eye*

THE

NAJAH LIGHTFOOT

FOREWORD BY JUDIKA ILLES

WEISER BOOKS

This edition first published in 2025 by Weiser Books, an imprint of
Red Wheel/Weiser, LLC
With offices at:
65 Parker Street, Suite 7
Newburyport, MA 01950
www.redwheelweiser.com

ISBN: 978-1-57863-885-7
Library of Congress Cataloging-in-Publication Data available upon request.

Cover and interior design by Sky Peck Design
Cover photograph by Anthony Camera
copyright © Najah Lightfoot
Interior photos, except where noted on pages 182–183, copyright © Najah Lightfoot

Typeset in Adobe Aldine
Printed in the United States of America
IBI
10 9 8 7 6 5 4 3 2 1

To my dolls who are always there . . .

Contents

Foreword, by Judika Illes *vii*

Acknowledgments *xv*

Introduction *1*

Chapter One. Inquiring Minds Want to Know *7*

Chapter Two. Spiritual Magic: Working with Dolls *43*

Chapter Three. Keeping Secrets: Initiating Your Doll *71*

Chapter Four. Hollywood Dolls *83*

Chapter Five. History of Dolls in Magick *121*

Chapter Six. Fascinating Doll Locations *139*

Chapter Seven. Personal Stories and Anecdotes *157*

In Conclusion *179*

Bibliography *181*

Photo Credits *182*

Foreword

I think I was born a doll lover. My mother was a lifelong doll lover, and she transmitted that love to me. I still have my childhood dolls and have now evolved into a collector of witch dolls, amassing a whole coven. I played with dolls, both by myself and with friends. We'd bring our dolls to play with each other. We staged doll weddings and celebrations. We played and the dolls played, too. But it went beyond play.

My mother and her sister sewed, crocheted, and beaded intricate outfits for my dolls. We created doll houses. When we traveled, we came home with souvenir dolls, evocative of a place and time. We read doll-themed books: Dare Wright's *The Lonely Doll* series, for example, and *Hitty: Her First Hundred Years* by Rachel Field, a novel told from a doll's perspective. Dolls are a culture and a world unto themselves and an ancient world at that. Let me take you on a little whirlwind tour of doll history.

To begin, let's examine what might be considered obvious: what exactly is a doll? Because of their ubiquity, it's easy to assume that *everyone* knows what dolls are, but they possess a complex, ancient, profound, and sometimes paradoxical history that may be unfamiliar to many. Merriam-Webster defines a doll as "a small-scale figure of a human being used especially as a child's plaything." Their small size, their strong associations with play and with children and especially with girl children, have led to dolls being frequently dismissed as trivial childish things, something to be

abandoned with maturity. However, this insistence on associating dolls solely with children's toys can blind us to their versatility and full power.

Doll history is human history. It is no exaggeration to describe them as among the earliest human creations. Anthropologists calculate that the earliest dolls may date back to the Paleolithic era—roughly 2.5 million years ago to 10,000 BCE, although, as so many were crafted from organic materials, their survival is rare.

As I write, what anthropologists now herald as the oldest documented surviving doll is estimated to be approximately 4,500 years old. Discovered in 2017 in a Bronze Age grave in Siberia, its head, just a few inches in size, was carved from soapstone, while the body was constructed from organic materials, which have deteriorated since its discovery. This Siberian doll is widely considered the oldest surviving doll precisely because of its discovery in a child's grave—it's presumed to be a plaything. But although we can recognize a humanoid form when we see one and identify the materials from which it was crafted and even carbon date it, we can't presume to know its original intended purpose.

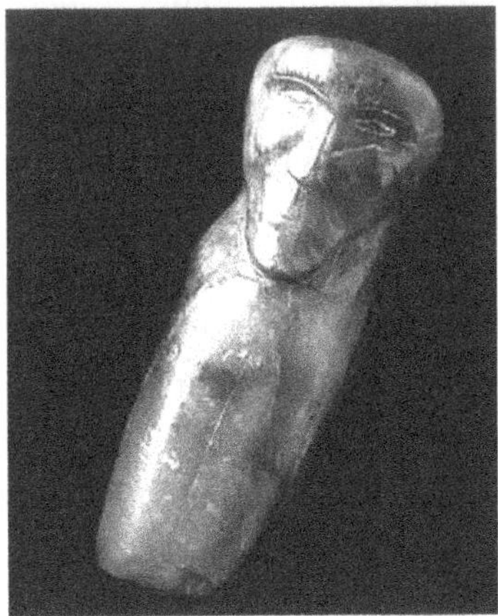

Oldest documented doll, 4,500 years old, bronze age.

The so-called Venus figurines of the Upper Paleolithic are also small, humanoid figures. The most famous, the Venus of Willendorf, is estimated to be about 30,000 years old. Carved from limestone, anthropologists do *not* consider her a child's plaything, although at just over four inches, she is only slightly larger than the Siberian doll. The Venus figurines are instead generally believed to be spiritual objects—idols, rather than dolls. Alternatively, they are considered magical tools intended to promote fertility.

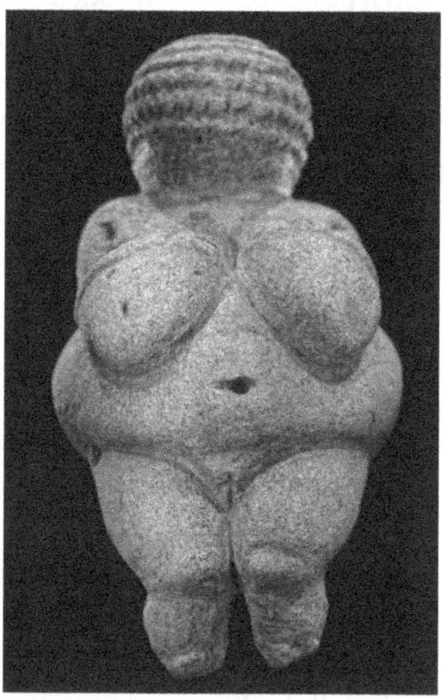

The Venus figurines, 30,000 years old, are generally believed to be spiritual objects rather than dolls.

Jōmon dogu figures are typically defined as "clay dolls." "Jōmon" refers to an ancient indigenous hunter-gatherer culture of Japan; the Jōmon era dates to approximately 14,000 to 300 BCE. They left behind mysterious humanoid, clay figurines: the dogu. These are occasionally classified

as playthings, but more frequently as religious statuary, possibly images of goddesses.

The dolls of ancient Egypt, Greece, Rome, and elsewhere are well documented. Ancient dolls are found even in regions that officially forbade "graven images" as can be attested by the literally countless unearthed small statuettes identified as the Hebrew goddess Lady Asherah.[1] The very commandment forbidding the making of graven images underscores the potential power of dolls. Wooden paddle dolls preserved in ancient Egyptian tombs, some with beautifully beaded hair, are dated back to 2000 BCE. Greek dolls with articulated (moveable) limbs date back to at least 200 BCE. Made from clay and wood, their moveable arms and legs connected to the torso with wire, they may be considered the ancestors of modern ball joint dolls.

An alabaster statuette with ruby eyes found near Babylon and dated to the third century BCE, also features moveable arms. Wearing a gold crescent moon crown and sporting another ruby in her navel, she was discovered in a family grave, positioned near the head of an adolescent girl.[2] She is widely considered a representation of a goddess, possibly Ishtar, Astarte, or Aphrodite. Whoever she is, it's fair to say she was intended as an eternal companion.

The versatility of dolls is breathtaking. Dolls *are* playthings and personal companions, but they also serve ritual, magical, spiritual, religious, divinatory, healing, and aesthetic purposes. Amuletic dolls provide protection, while talismanic dolls beckon good fortune. Nang Kwak, a Thai goddess of prosperity, is typically venerated in the guise of a small figurine. Dolls are modern therapy tools. Used now, as in the past, to teach

1 For more information, see Raphael Patai's book *The Hebrew Goddess* (Wayne State University Press, 1990).

2 Stephanie M. Langin-Hooper, "A Girl's Helping Hand on the Journey to the Afterlife: Alabaster Ishtar–Aphrodite Figurines from Seleucid-Parthian Babylonia," *Ancient Near East Today* 11, no. 12 (December 2023), *anetoday.org/langin-hooper-figurines-babylonia.*

childrearing, dolls are also investigative tools, sometimes used similarly to mugshots.

Dolls—especially styles of dolls—have evolved to represent nations. *Matryoshka* dolls, painted wooden nesting dolls with progressively smaller dolls fitting snugly insider larger ones, represent Russia (although their roots are in Japan, a nation with an exceptionally rich doll culture). The *Akua'ba* doll, typically carved from wood into an ankh-like shape, was initially intended to stimulate fertility via spiritual and magical means. Although still used in this manner, the Akua'ba also serves as an emblem of Ghana, even appearing on Ghanaian postage stamps.

Matryoshka dolls.

According to the animistic philosophy inherent in Shintoism, the native religion of Japan, *everything* has a soul. Dolls, in particular, because of their resemblance to humans, possess consciousness, as well. Thus, if a doll cannot be kept, it cannot simply be disposed of carelessly. At the

very least, this is considered disrespectful, while at worst, it encourages bad luck and may be a spiritual transgression, as well as possibly attracting retribution from the doll. There is a solution: dolls may be sent to the Awashima Shrine for correct ritual disposal. Founded in the fourth century, it is the head shrine of approximately one thousand Awashima shrines in Japan. It is also the birthplace of the annual doll festival held on March 3rd, the *Hinamatsuri.*[3]

That's just the tip of the iceberg of doll history around the world. I'm jumping from place to place and era to era, but dolls are our shared human heritage and always have been.

Najah Lightfoot has written a unique, magical, and powerful book. Plenty of books explore doll history or teach you how to craft types of dolls or catalog their current financial worth. But to the best of my knowledge, there is no other book like *The Spiritual Magic of Dolls,* one that expressly explores the bonds of love and companionship shared between dolls and people. Through her words and by her example, Najah teaches us how to cultivate strong, healthy, and respectful relationships with our dolls. If you have inherited dolls, possess special dolls, or simply feel drawn to dolls, Najah can show you how to develop the profound and deep bonds that have kept dolls our constant companions for millennia. She demonstrates how dolls can help heal us and—especially in the case of haunted dolls— how we can help heal them.

A basic tenet of magic is that coincidences don't exist or at least not as mere random happenings. Although not every "coincidence" is equally significant, what they do is indicate that something has significance and deserves our attention.

As it turns out, the days during which I wrote and completed this foreword held special significance for me, as they coincide with the anniversary of my mother's death. The last gift I ever gave her was a doll. In addition, the great singer David Johansen, last surviving member of the

3 "Of Dolls and Underpants: Awashima Shrine," *japantravel.navitime.com.*

prototypical New York City rock band The New York Dolls and among my favorites, died during the writing. The passing of the last of the Dolls, while I was writing this foreword, leads me to ponder the deeper nuances of the word 'doll', once a casual and common term of endearment in the New York in which I grew up.

Last, but not least, I find myself completing this foreword on March 3, the date of the Hinamatsuri, Japan's doll festival—a sacred day for dolls and those who love them. These coincidences emphasize for me the importance and necessity of *The Spiritual Magic of Dolls.* Najah Lightfoot has created a portal to enhance, empower, and enable your own sacred relationships with your dolls. May this book help bring you endless joy and fulfillment.

—Judika Illes, author of *Encyclopedia of 5,000 Spells,*
Encyclopedia of Spirits, and other books of magic
March 3, 2025

Acknowledgements

It takes a village to raise a book. Making the decision to write a book, whether it is your first, second, or third book, can take days, hours, months, and sometimes years to birth into being. It all starts with a flickering idea, a sliver in your brain, a gnawing feeling that you have something to say. You have a desire to communicate and share experiences, which you feel you must commit to paper, in the hopes your words may help someone who is on a similar journey to know they are not alone. A book is not created in a vacuum.

I would like to thank the following people, for their continuing encouragement and support of my work as a writer:

My family: my dear hubby Tim Bagley, our wonderful adult children, and grandchildren; Robert Herrmann, Eric and Kelly Williams, Camden, Cainen, Chloe, Jazmin, and our sweet dog, Terra, who is always by my side. From my heart of hearts to all of you, your love and support mean the world to me. Hugs, hugs, hugs.

To Judika Illes, my editor, for her encouragement, excitement, and enthusiasm, to Kathryn Sky-Peck for her incredible, stunning cover design, to Priestess Stephanie Rose Bird for being there when I needed a mentor and support, to Judy Martindale for her quiet, behind the scenes encouragement and appreciation, to Lois Harvey and Matt Aragon-Shafi of West Side Books for continuing to operate one of the

best real bookstores on the planet and always letting me know you see me, to Jasmine Williams, Cynthia Conti-Cook, Michael Wahlin, for sharing their personal stories, to Kat Neff, who loves dolls, to Jesse Bransford and Pam Grossman for giving me the invitation of a lifetime, by inviting me to speak and teach about my dolls at the 2023 NYU Occult Humanities Conference, to Gretchen and Rich Ashburn my most dear darling magical friends, who are family in heart and soul to me, to Toni Rotonda, and Steven Intermill of the Buckland Museum of Witchcraft for their wondrous friendship and maintaining the stories of witches, to Kat Tigner, my fairy witch goddess mother, to Charlene Cheech White for her laughter, amazing strength and tattoo artistry, to Kara Seal, my dear incredible librarian and friend, to Terry Iacuzzo, for her incomparable insight and gifts, to Ricardo Pustanio, visionary, master creator and sculptor, to Clifford Hartleigh Low for his New York magic and friendship, to Markus Ironwood, I send a big hug, to Cairelle Crow Perilloux, for creating the magic of the first New Orleans Witches' Ball, to my dolls, who believe in me and my work, to my Mom, Halimah Shaheed, who gave me my first Black baby doll in 1964, and to the incredibly, magically talented and masterful, photographer Anthony Camera, for his ability to capture the magic of me and my dolls, through the lens of his camera.

To all the amazing people who shared their stories with me and attended my doll classes at Between the Worlds: Sacred Space Conference 2023, Mystic South Conference 2023, and NYU Occult Humanities Conference 2023, I thank you.

To my dearly beloved Aunt Bette Smith-Milne who passed from this life on November 01, 2022. I will forever hold you in my heart. Not a day goes by that I don't remember you and miss you. Your legacy, love and support are always with me.

To all the above your inspiration means more to me than you may ever know. I hope you can feel it through the words on these pages.

To the Denver Center for Performing Arts Education Department, the Robert and Judi Newman Center, lovingly known as DCPA, thank you for being my happy place, my portal, my place of making my dreams come true, and showing me, it's real.

To all the wonderful people and places who follow and support me on Instagram, Facebook and YouTube, I see you. Thank you, thank you, thank you!

Introduction

They stare at me. I feel them when I walk into a store. They call to me from movies, television shows and films. I am attracted to them, and they know it. They know they will be safe with me; they know I'll try to help others understand them, get comfortable with them, or find them better homes. They know if something isn't right for them, I'll feel it, and try my best to pass along the information.

They know I'm not scared of them, even if some of them are created to be scary and elicit uncomfortable feelings. They know I understand that not all of them should come home with you or be your friend. They know *I listen to them.*

On my social media feed, a picture of a doll appeared in what was listed as a haunted place, an asylum with a long and painful history. The doll in the photo sat on an abandoned tricycle. She was dirty and she looked very sad.

According to the post, the place where the photos were taken is afflicted with sorrow, as it was a place that did not do well by its inhabitants. Of course, the first photo posted is of a doll, long discarded and forgotten, and the comments regarding the doll were not kind.

I did not comment on the photo. But my heart went out the doll. Immediately I wanted to offer to have them send the doll to me. In this place, now riddled with painful memories and horrible tragedies, she may

have been a child's only friend. Now, through the eyes of social media, she has dispersions and fear cast upon her, subjected to fear-based perceptions because she was left behind as a witness to horrible events. Granted, most people would run screaming from the room if they saw this doll in person. She affected me differently when I looked at her photo in my newsfeed. I had a longing to help her.

This longing I feel when I look at dolls, this *gift* I have to connect with them, is why I felt the need to write this book.

As humans, we impart our perspectives and our life experiences upon dolls. If our lives have been happy and relatively free from trauma and pain, we tend to see our dolls in the same light. However, if we have experienced trauma, psychic, or physical or emotional, we may also transfer those feelings to our dolls. Some dolls can take hold of those feelings for decades, perhaps even centuries. Other dolls may not have been created to function as emotional supports, but they have a role in bringing joy and happiness to their families or owners nonetheless. Other dolls may have been created to fuel our imaginations with scary thoughts, or instead they may lift our spirits with imaginative whimsies of a happy day spent at a tea party with all our best friends.

Either way, dolls exist as our friends and confidants. They are so much more than simple mass-manufactured items or handstitched and hand-painted heirlooms. If you feel called to dolls, if you find yourself desiring to have deeper relationships with them, then may I invite you to turn the page and journey with me into the spiritual magic of dolls?

Why Dolls?

In April of 2023, I was a featured presenter at Between the Worlds: Sacred Space Conference, in Baltimore, MD. I was asked to teach three workshops. For my first two classes I presented material from my second book *Powerful Juju: Goddesses, Music & Magic for Comfort, Guidance & Protection.*

My workshops were a hit. Everyone seemed to get a lot of information and affirmation from our time together. It was fun and exhilarating to teach material from my book.

When I submitted material for my classes to the conference organizers, they impressed upon me that their conference was geared toward practitioners who had many years of experience in their fields, and as such, many writers, teachers, and speakers found they could use the conference to try out new material. How fun! As featured presenters, we would be required to teach three classes. The classes could be rituals, classes or workshops, or a combination of all three. My first two classes were of the ritual and workshop nature.

However, for my third class, I decided to step out of my comfort zone, and teach material on a subject which is near and dear to me. That subject is the spiritual magic of working with *dolls*.

I can't really say why this subject seemed to call my name, a class I thought might be well received with the attendees at the Between the Worlds: Sacred Space conference, but I felt, because of the way the organizers spoke about the level of proficiency of the conference attendees and the opportunity to test out new material, that I would give teaching about dolls and my relationship with them a shot. Spiritually speaking, sharing about my experiences with dolls is something that has been present with me for a long time.

As a magical person who writes books and contributes to periodicals and to the books of others (an experience for which I am truly grateful), I also find that it's good to challenge myself when it comes to teaching and sharing different subjects, especially in front of a live audience. Public speaking is one of the most common things people list among their greatest fears. My desire to reach new levels of confidence by speaking in front of people and sharing with new people is something that both scares and excites me. I also like discussing unusual or niche topics people may not expect would interest me.

As a mercurial Gemini, my creative mind enjoys exploring different subjects. I thrive on learning new things and adventures. My curiosity to explore and share what I have experienced is one of my greatest strengths. I try not to become pigeon-holed or stereotyped. I don't like to feel typecast as one particular kind of writer, magical practitioner, spiritual person, or witch. There is room for everybody. We all have something to contribute and bring to the table, and that's something I endeavor to embody in my teaching.

As I began to prepare for my classes, I found myself having doubts. Even though I knew I would be teaching at a conference filled with open-minded, inquisitive people who are interested in a lot of different subjects, including many subjects that spiral out from what many consider more traditional occult knowledge and the different esoteric and magical traditions, I wasn't quite sure how my dollie class would be received. Dolls are divisive. It's common knowledge that people either love dolls and love talking about them and sharing their personal stories about them, or they run screaming from the room at the mere mention of them. After all, there's a reason why so many horror movies star dolls.

(Of course, I am among those in the first category. I love dolls and I love *my dolls*. And my dolls are not just any dolls, my dolls are *super special*. I will introduce you to a select few of them in these pages, the ones who have given their permission for me to include them in this book. They are excited to help people get closer to their dolls and have better relationships with them.)

I also decided as I prepared my class material it would be important to me spiritually, as a magical person and a witch, to discuss the differences between the kinds of dolls people normally associate with the occult or magical practices—such as poppets, clay dolls, target dolls, and "Voodoo" dolls—and the type of dolls which come to me to become part of my magical life and my beloved family members.

Although in this book I will also discuss dolls that are commonly associated with the occult, my primary focus is not on the practices of using dolls for harmful or baneful magic. This book is about the wonder, awe, and love one has for dolls, and how to incorporate their presence into your life, should you wish to develop a deeper relationship with them.

As of this writing, I have now taught my dollie class three times; once in Baltimore at the Between the Worlds: Sacred Spaces Conference 2023, at the Mystic South Conference 2023 in Atlanta, Georgia in, and the Occult Humanities Conference 2023 at NYU in New York City. My dolls and I were on the circuit in 2023, and for those experiences I will be forever grateful!

My presentations were well received, far beyond my expectations. I was touched at how many people couldn't wait to tell me about their beloved dolls—people ranging in age from grandparents to young people. It quickly spread throughout the conferences that I was "the doll person." People would say to me, "Oh, you're teaching that class on dolls!"

The Emotional Reaction to Dolls

At the conferences I presented at, people would react to the topic of my doll class in one of two ways: they would either want to talk to me, or they would get a bit shaken.

It's not uncommon for people to be afraid of dolls. There's even a word for it: pediophobia. I completely respect people's feelings about dolls. In fact, I'm the type who, if I were in a group of people speaking about the subject and I noticed someone was becoming uncomfortable, I would decline to discuss the topic any further. I'm not into pushing people's buttons just to get a reaction or using the topic of dolls to shock or scare them. Plus, behaving in that manner is disrespectful to my love of dolls.

We all have things that creep us out. I never push the subject or topic of dolls upon people who are frightened of or indifferent to dolls. It's very clear when people have a fear of dolls, or when they are not interested in the subject. It shows on their faces and in their body language. However, those of us who do love dolls enjoy talking about them and sharing personal stories. Many would like to get to know their dolls better. This book will show you how to better get to know your own dolls, as well as how to work with them spiritually.

After my doll classes were over, the response I received was fantastic. Many people told me that my class was one of their favorites. They told me how much they appreciated the material, and some people even brought their own dolls to meet me and my dollies!

So, if you're curious about working with dolls, or have a love of dolls and want to explore engaging working with them magically, please read on!

Blessings!

—Najah Lightfoot

CHAPTER ONE

Inquiring Minds Want to Know

Dolls are just for children. Dolls are toys. Dolls have no meaning beyond their clothing, or the space they take up on a shelf. Adults who like dolls are weird. I would never keep dolls in my house. Dolls are *evil.*

What?!

Yes, it's true. Many people feel that way about dolls. Just thinking about dolls creeps them out. Taking it further, talking to your dolls, and interacting with dolls, can seem especially strange as one gets older and leaves the realm of childhood make-believe and imagination behind.

But isn't that the cornerstone of all magic? Isn't that what makes ritual magick so profound? (We'll explore more about the difference between *magic* and *magick* later in this book.) Does everything need a scientific explanation for it to be true? Aren't there things still unexplained in the Universe?

Aren't our childlike awe and wonder portals to the great beyond, beyond?

Let me give you a personal example. I love the old Sinbad movies from 1958. I've taught myself the words to summon the genie:

"From the land beyond, beyond,
from the world past hope and fear,
I bid you genie now appear!"

I believe in the genie, and I believe in the magic lamp. I don't need to see them or touch them physically to know that they're real. I don't want to live in a world where everything is predicated on what I can see with my two physical eyes, and touch with my two hands. It would be a sad day indeed for me to believe that, as human beings, we've discovered everything there is to know about the Universe, and the worlds of seen and unseen. There just has to be more. I know it. I feel it!

Dolls live in the in-between worlds. They exist in magical and magickal realms. They exude the certain presence of beings who are not actually alive, but at the same time *feel* imbued with a life force. They fuel our imaginations and uplift our hearts.

Dolls are record keepers. They exist in time and outside of time. They are mirrors that look back and forth simultaneously. If you know the creation date of an old doll, she can take you back to that time when you gaze into her eyes. She can share with you all she has seen and experienced, if you are willing to listen. A new doll created in present time can open you to the creation of new possibilities, new adventures and the future. One very interesting property about dolls is they appear to remain the same age as they were created, for example, a baby doll or a child's doll will always *look* like a baby or a child, but chronologically they could be very old. Magic!

It is these undeniable connections and stirring emotions that place dolls in the categories of magic and magick. It is the awe and wonder dolls bring to the lives of countless people who know they have power and meaning, who connect with them in ways that whisper unto their hearts. But what is magic? What is magick? What is the difference indicated by one simple letter? Read on to discover for yourself.

Magic versus Magick

It's a new day. The sun rises and a beam of a light shoots across the morning sky. Colors beyond explanation flood the heavens. White clouds may float by. A bird may sing its morning song, or a bunny may hop down the street. Doggie walkers may pass by and stop to greet you. You have a feeling that anything and everything is possible.

How do you start your day? You may say prayers, perform rituals, or find ways to express your love and gratitude for a new day and a new beginning. You may turn and face the directions of east, south, west, and north. Or you may raise your hands in a gesture of gratitude and thanksgiving. The light of a new day has stirred your soul.

Hours have passed. The morning which awakened you is long past, and the daylight hours are ending. It is now evening time. The sun is setting, and the moon begins to rise. Transcendent colors of pink, orange, and deep yellow are painting the western sky. Depending upon the time of year or your location, you may be able to witness the moon beginning to climb in the sky. Seeing the moon rise can be an awe-inspiring event. Whether it be the first crescent of the moon, the moon going through phases—new, waxing or waning—or coming into itself as the full moon, which is certainly an auspicious time, these moments can heighten your senses.

Or perhaps it's midnight and you hear the "quork" of a raven or the hoot of an owl as it flies silently through the night sky. Or maybe a thunderstorm sends cracking lightning, shattering the silence and breaking open the portal of night. It could also be the soft pitter-patter of rain that gently lulls you to sleep and gives you enchanting dreams.

All these things define *magic*. You can't explain it, but it does something to your soul. It makes you feel good. It stirs your emotions and brings a smile to your face. It lifts your spirits. What's even better is you haven't done anything to will or bring the experience into being. You have

simply seen, felt, and or acknowledged it. It has caught your attention. Your awareness of the moment and your ability to recognize it has made it so. It's magic!

What else is magic? Maybe your heart has skipped a beat, because you're in love. You're deeply, crazily attracted to someone, and you have no idea why you have feelings for them. You just know when you're in their presence that life is better. You can't stop thinking about them. Or maybe you just watched a movie, a play, or a television show and you're crying your eyes out. You need a tissue. Your mind and soul have journeyed to places long forgotten, or you've remembered or recalled moments in your life that are incredibly special to you. You may feel nostalgic or melancholy. Sometimes it's good to cry.

Maybe a new song has stirred your soul, or an old favorite tune has played through your air pods, headphones, or Bluetooth speakers, catching you totally off-guard, when you least expected it, and now you are lost in time, reliving or revisiting tender feelings that were perhaps long forgotten. Or maybe the music has enticed you, seduced you into future thoughts and dreams you may not have realized or manifested into reality. An ethereal portal has opened and you've entered it.

Do you believe in magic? Yes. Yes, you do.

Now, let's change direction. Picture that, perhaps, it is the time and cycle of the new moon, when the moon is increasing in size from the sliver of the crescent moon to the round, full moon. You've decided you're going to consciously set intentions to bring increase and abundance into your life. You're going to say words of affirmation, light some candles, burn some incense. You may decide to write those words of affirmation on paper, roll the paper up, tie it up with a pretty ribbon or string, and consciously hold it. You might look at it for several days, or place it on your altar to seal your intentions and manifest your desires into reality.

It might be the time of the Winter Solstice or Spring Equinox. Perhaps it is the highly spiritual and sensitive time of the autumn season, and you feel the whispers and callings of those who have crossed over or gone before you.

You have learned through your practices that these times of the year are auspicious for doing and performing dedicated works. You may spend days or weeks gathering items to support your intentions. You may decide you need to wear special clothes or robes. You may invite others to join you.

You pick out a time and place where you will not be disturbed. In your workings you may use tools of divination, such as tarot cards, a pendulum, or oracle cards. You may light a fire, sing, chant, or inscribe words on paper or candles specific to your ceremony. You've considered this ceremony for a long time. You have not come lightly to this moment. A feeling of excitement and anticipation courses through you.

It is now the time of the waning moon. You've decided this is a good time to set intentions and do work to let go of things which no longer serve you, or habits you wish discard. You are ready to make serious changes in your life. You may have written out your intentions on paper. You may consider lighting the paper on fire and burying the ashes. You may choose to stay home and flush the strong emotions you have written out on paper down the toilet. You may have consulted your tools of divination or asked your Higher Power for guidance as you go into the night of the waning moon to let go of that which is disturbing your peace and serenity. You've thought long and hard about what you are going to do and prepared yourself to be strong and courageous. You may go to the crossroads or a cemetery at night to leave offerings and ask the Spirits for their help in aiding you during your time of need.

This is *magick*. This is the act of performing intentional deeds to affect our lives in positive ways, whether they be for healing, to let go, to discard what we no longer need or serves us, or to seek protection for

ourselves, our family, our friends, or loved ones. We have decided we need spiritual intervention and assistance from our Higher Power. We are willing and committed to doing the work. We are ready and prepared to step forward. We are ready to perform acts of magick.

Dolls, Magic, and Magick

How do our dolls fit into the worlds of magic versus magick?

Dolls by their very nature convey a magical presence. When you look at them, hold them, sleep with them, cry with them, whisper to them, and tell them your secrets, they automatically lift your spirits and convey trust. You haven't done anything to elicit these feelings. These feelings seem to magically appear.

These emotional connections arise in your soul and spirit and make you feel better, similar to the emotions you feel when you gaze upon the morning sun, watch the full moon rise, or listen to your favorite song. It is your awareness, your innate calling, and our human connection to nature. No one needs to define or explain why you look at the sun, moon, and stars, or keep returning to your favorite playlist. We appreciate these things as they are, for what they are, the touchstones of the days and nights of our lives. These spectacular moments do not decrease in wonder simply because they occur on a daily basis, or the mere fact we can access them with the touch of a keyboard or button.

In fact, we take relief and solace knowing the sun will rise, night will come. The stars do shine night after night, and the music will always be there. We know, we trust, even through the darkest nights or when the shadows come to call, that the morning light will come, music will soothe and comfort, and a new day will dawn upon the earth.

Our dolls live in liminal, emotional moments of time. They quietly exist, sitting and waiting for us to return to them when we need them. They stand by like sentries guarding a secret door which you can only

These twin dollies came to town with a friend to visit.

access by holding them, touching them, being with them. Many of us have found comfort during dark times in our lives, dark nights of the soul, or times of trauma by connecting to and being with our dolls. They provide their own special brand of emotional support. One of their best qualities is that they excel at communicating without actually speaking. They listen to us, and they hear our words and our troubles without judgement. This is their special magic. (Maybe we need to invent "emotional support" vests for our dolls!)

What if you decide you need your dolls to go one step further? What if you need your doll to step up into a greater role and assist you in a working, or take an active role in ritual or ceremony, such as setting

intentions for increase during a waxing moon cycle, or to help you let go of things which no longer serve you during a waning moon cycle?

If this is something you desire for your dolls, your dolls will have entered into a magickal experience with you. They become active participants in your magickal spell work, rituals, or ceremonies. Your dolls can do and be both things: magical and magickal.

It is up to you to decide how they come into these spaces by developing an ongoing relationship with them. One of the best things dolls have in an unlimited capacity is time. Time is what develops your connection to them and allows you to ascertain how they may become, or if they should become allies in your magickal work.

It is also totally acceptable if you never feel comfortable bringing your dolls into magickal workings. Some dolls are not designed for that purpose. When you are attuned to dolls, and specific dolls come into your life, you may already know what purpose they serve. Some dolls by design naturally love to sit and be admired. Some dolls may have elaborate clothing you do not wish to disturb, and some dolls may be very old and touching and holding them may be detrimental to their longevity. However, there are other dolls who are very suited to participating in magickal ritual.

I have lots of dolls. Not all of them participate in magickal workings with me. In all honesty, it is only a select few that attend rituals and rites and travel with me to conferences. I know through the trusted relationship I have developed with them that they enjoy these events. They like being in sacred space, as well as meeting new people.

A lot of my dolls simply give and reflect the love I have for them. I enjoy being with my dolls, taking care of them, talking to them, sharing space with them, dusting them from time to time, and blessing them. As a doll person, you will come to know the relationship between you and your dolls, as they become part of your life.

Dolls are special. Since they are created in the images of human beings, they already contain magical or may contain magickal properties within them. It will be up to you and your dolls to decide which path they are best suited. Some dolls can be both magical and magickal!

Malevolent Dolls

I can hear the question you're asking: What if a doll appears to have a malevolent nature? Well, if your senses are tingling, this may be a possibility for the doll you behold. The next step you will need to take is to decide if you are ready or willing to *embrace* that nature of your doll.

A doll which gives off this type of malevolent or frightening vibe can test you. It is easy to feel this vibe when you encounter a doll that was created to be scary. You may need to stop and ask yourself some questions. A doll may *look* scary, but is it truly malevolent? Is it simply a spooky Halloween doll, crafted in fun for the season? Or is it a doll you've found on its own, sitting and waiting for a new home? When you look at it, does it scare you? You can usually recognize a doll that has been made or used for nefarious purposes, especially as you begin to build your "dollie senses." The vibe just doesn't seem right. Something in your gut tells you to step away.

If a doll genuinely frightens you, ask yourself: Are you prepared to bring that type of doll into your home? Are you prepared to do the type of work to protect the doll and yourself, should you decide to work with the doll in such a magickal manner?

As long as dolls have existed, which is centuries and centuries, going back to the first person who created a stick image of a human being, folkloric history tells us people have created dolls to use for baneful, malevolent purposes. *That is not our focus nor the intention of this book.*

We are instead focused on the types of dolls you may find in an antique store, at an estate sale, or perhaps that someone gifted to you

thinking you may be the right person for the doll. The doll wants to be with you, and you wish to become that dollie's person.

If you and the doll you're considering bringing home are at odds, if the doll gives you creepy vibes or disturbs you, or if you look at the doll and feel unsettled by its presence, I suggest not bringing it home. Not all dolls are meant to be family members. Sometimes you just have to say, "Thank you but no thank you!" and leave the doll be. There is no need to try and rescue every single doll you see. It is highly possible there are many dolls for whom you may not be their "person." Don't feel bad if you don't feel called to be the "person," to every doll that crosses your path. There are so many, many dolls in the world. The right doll will come to you, in its own way, in its own time.

A doll should make you feel good, lift your spirits and lighten your being. It should emote the feelings you experience when you make a new friend, you're excited about going on a new adventure, or you've just found the perfect pair of shoes. It should elicit a gasp of joy!

If, over time after building a relationship with your doll, you choose to bring the doll into a magickal working, your doll will become a comfort, like a trusted sentry guarding your secrets. Remember to treat your dolls with love and respect, and they will do the same for you.

A Doll's Home

I have many dolls in my collection. Each doll has their own space to call home. Some live on top of a dresser, some live in my office, others may hide in special places or reside on our front porch, in our back yard, or even on our mantle. The more dolls you have the more necessary it becomes to find spaces for them to call home.

It's important for dolls to have places they can call their own, just like our human family members. That doesn't mean they must live in one space permanently. At times you may find the need to move them from

one spot to another, but they will always have a dedicated spot. Dolls can outgrow a space, just like a person may outgrow their room or home. As you develop a relationship with your dolls, you may find they fit better in a different room, shelf, or dwelling area.

I've had some of my dolls since childhood. Others have been gifted to me. Some dolls hang together in groups, others not so much. Sometimes you will want a doll to live in a space with your other dolls, and no matter how hard you try, it just won't happen. You may notice you place the doll with your other dolls and when you return or look back, the doll is slumped over or refuses to stand upright. That is a sign that the doll needs a different space to live. No need to try and force the issue. Find a new space for the doll, one where she will be comfortable.

Let me give you some examples of a doll's space. Three of my dolls have become a core group to each other. They are always together. They live together in a magical basket. If I move them, they move in their basket. Their basket is their home, and they feel safe and comfortable within it.

Several of my older Black dolls exist together on a shelf. I don't add any dolls to that group, although when a new doll comes into my life, I always introduce the doll to my older Black dolls, as a gesture of respect for being my elder dolls. They are the matriarchs of my doll family, even though some of them were created to represent babies or children. A baby doll can be a very old doll. One of my most precious dolls is a baby doll. However, I've had her since 1964! Even though she looks and will always look like a baby, she is actually sixty-one years old. A few more years and she will be eligible for Social Security!

One thing you will learn when you begin to work with dolls is if you *listen* to them, they will tell you where they belong, what makes them feel comfortable, and what type of work, if any, they are willing to do, or feel most comfortable doing.

Haunted versus Presence

Not every doll is haunted, although I would venture to say that all dolls have a *presence,* some more so than others.

By the sheer creation of making a doll, a doll has a presence. Somewhere, somehow, a human being fashioned in their mind the image for the doll. The doll came into being, manifested into reality by the work of human hands, or machines created by humans, to make the doll represent a human adult, child, or baby.

The mere fact a doll resembles a human being gives it energy, solidity, and in some cases an eerie quality. Perhaps that is why many people shriek at the sight of dolls. They look too much like us or someone we may have known. They tap into recognition, or they fuel our imaginations with images of how we may like to appear.

Dolls stir unexplainable emotions. Those emotions can be quite difficult for some people to handle, especially if the person has a fear of dolls, or dolls make them uncomfortable.

Some dolls are handmade, with each body part lovingly stitched, real hair wigs attached to the head, shoes made in precise measurements to fit the feet, clothes exceptionally designed for that doll, all put together by its creator. An internet search for doll clothing will return a plethora of information. Clothing for dolls is its own cottage industry. Collectors value the originality and authenticity of the clothes a doll is wearing.

(My husband and I love watching *The Antiques Road Show.* You can gain so much knowledge about dolls, their history, and their value just by watching a few episodes. Dolls matter! I've actually tried a few times to get on the show. I came close one year, but Covid reared its ugly head, and the show went on hiatus, like the rest of life during that time. Several years later when the show announced it was returning to Colorado, I tried again, but alas I did not make it. I'll keep trying. It could happen! I would love to have one of my dolls appear on the show.)

An 1880's French porcelain doll in intricately tailored ivory dress/iStock

Other dolls emerge from factories, where their body parts are pulled from giant crates, waiting on assembly for mass production. In doll factories, there are crates and rooms that house each body part for a doll, as the doll is assembled. It is indeed a macabre environment. Doll heads in one area, arms and legs in another, eyeballs in buckets, hair pieces waiting to be stitched or glued to the doll's head. It is a bit freaky!

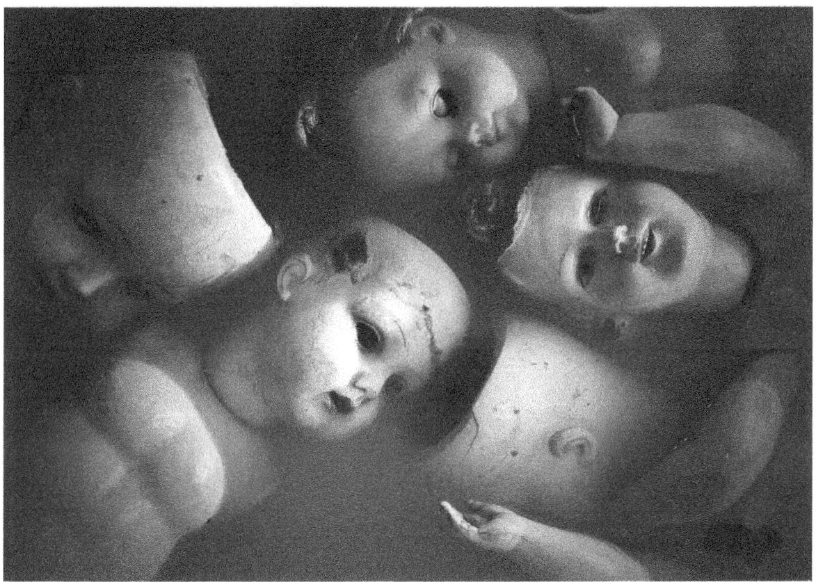

Dolls waiting to be made fully whole.

Knowing factory-made dolls sit around, just waiting for their body parts to be attached, may contribute to why dolls freak a lot of people out. Just thinking about that imagery is like a mini horror movie playing in your mind. The head hangs on a hook waiting to be attached, the eyeballs get picked up and glued inside the socket, the arm gets attached, and the mouth gets painted with some awful lipstick color.

Sometimes you may find you can't or just don't want to look at a doll. Did its eyes move? Are the eyes following you around the room? Is the head in a different position from the last time you saw it? Did it *really* move, or are you imagining it? Is one piece of clothing in a different place since the last time you looked at it?

It's completely possible all of those things happened, but that doesn't necessarily mean the doll is haunted. It could simply mean your doll is trying to communicate with you. Don't be afraid. Listen. Pick up your doll and hold it close to you. How do you feel when you hold it? Do you feel better? Do you get warm and fuzzy feelings from your doll when you pick it up?

A lot of times what people misconstrue as a doll being haunted is the doll simply wanting to establish companionship. That is their purpose. They were created to be hugged, loved, and admired. They want to become part of the family. They seek to be played with, carried around, talked to as a friend or beloved family member. They want to be a part of the life of the person, or persons, into whose lives they have come. They like to hang out with you when you're having your morning cup of coffee, spending time writing in your journal, or being creative. When you realize this about dolls, that they are simply trying to serve their purpose, this may help to alleviate any creepy feelings you may experience when you are in their presence.

Now, a haunted doll is different.

A haunted doll gives off a vibe that you immediately recognize as foreign. Do you recoil from it when you approach it? If holding it, do you have an overwhelming sensation to put it down as quickly as possible?

Do you get a weird sensation in your gut that makes you want to run from the room? The emotional reaction you feel when you look at a haunted doll is visceral.

You have absolutely no desire to hug the doll, touch it, or carry it home with you. The feeling is personal, and it feels intrusive, as if

the doll is trying to enter your space without your permission. For example, one of my favorite movies is *The Fifth Element,* a 1977 sci-fi film starring Bruce Willis and Milla Jovovich. In one scene, Bruce Willis's character, Korben Dallas, brings Leeloo, played by Milla Jovovich, to meet the priest. While waiting for the priest to appear, Korben tries to kiss Leeloo.

Leeloo's reaction is palpable. She speaks fiercely to Korben in her divine language as a Supreme Being. Korben doesn't understand what she has said, and asks the priest to interpret for him. The priest tells him Leeloo basically said "not without my permission."

To me, this perfectly describes the interaction we may have when we come into the presence of a haunted doll. Immediately our defenses go up. We feel as if someone or something is trying to invade us, to encroach upon us without our consent. Magical, spiritual people are highly intuitive. People in general are blessed with flight or fight wiring for our protection. Pay attention to those feelings if you find yourself experiencing them in the presence of a doll.

One of the best TV shows to present a creepy, haunted, spooky, doll is the "Living Doll ~ Talky Tina" episode from the *Twilight Zone* series, which aired November 1st, 1963. I also found it interesting that the name of the character who plays the "Mother," is Annabelle. It seems the name Annabelle has a long history of being associated with creepy things. In this episode the doll becomes a protector to the little girl, taking her job to extreme levels of protection.

Should you come into contact with a haunted doll, it is highly possible the reaction you may experience is not the same reaction others may have when they look at the doll. Haunted energy is known to attach itself in singular threads. Two people can stand in front of a "haunted," doll and have completely different experiences. One may experience disturbing, unsettling emotions, while the other person may have no reactions or feel nothing untoward. A lot of our reactions to

dolls come from our past experiences and how we may feel about dolls in general. Also, many dolls can sense how *you feel about them.* Most dolls are created to give and receive love. However, dolls do exist that come from places or people who may have not had the best intentions for the doll.

As witches and magical, spiritual people, we must learn to trust our gut and our intuition. Trusting our gut and our magical sensations is a skill we develop over time. We build strength, power, and confidence by listening to our nudges and hunches.

Do you feel instantly better when you remove yourself from the presence of the doll? If so, you can be sure you've made the right decision. If something gives you the heebie-jeebies, and/or you sense a malevolent or untoward presence from an object, then I suggest you stay far away from it!

It's also possible you may purchase or bring home a doll who, over time, starts to change. It's possible that what started out being a lovely relationship with your doll, one you found yourself drawn to, now suddenly becomes a doll you don't enjoy. It is totally okay if you and the doll need to part ways. It doesn't necessarily mean the doll is haunted. It could just mean you and the doll have outgrown each other. Trying to re-home dolls you've outgrown is a nice way to give the doll a chance to be loved by someone else.

There are plenty of places and things, including dolls, with which I have no desire to make a connection. I know there may be people who feel they can bring home a doll who they know has a sketchy history or who people have described as "haunted." It's totally possible there are people who can work with items many others would never touch. Some people are gifted in that manner, and they know how to handle themselves in the presence of "questionable" heirlooms, items, and dolls. Hats off to those people!

My latest doll came to me at an Oddities and Curiosities show. It took me over an hour to decide if she was really the doll for me. I found myself deeply attracted to her at first glance, but my intuition told me to walk away, give it some time, and return later.

It wasn't that I felt she was haunted; she was just very different from all my other dolls. Eventually, after giving it much thought, by walking around the Oddities and Curiosities show and looking at lots of bizarre and creepy items, I decided to return to the seller and see if she was still there waiting for me. She was. I decided to bring her home and add her to our family. I'm so glad I did. She has become a great source of comfort and a friend.

Dolls can also become haunted due to their environment. Just like the phrase "they're a product of their environment," the same is true with dolls. Dolls absorb energy, especially old, vintage, or discarded dolls. A new doll fresh out of the package is like a newborn baby. It is ready to be imprinted with love and affection from its surroundings.

An old doll, or a discarded doll, has seen much and been through a lot of living. If you are drawn to old dolls or discarded dolls, when you bring them home, think about them in the same respect as you would a rescued animal, or one you adopt from a shelter. You know the animal you're bringing into your life has had many experiences, and these experiences, even if you don't know directly what they are, have had an impact on your rescue. You don't try to force your rescued shelter animal into doing things or being in spaces that make it uncomfortable. In fact, it's just the opposite. You do everything in your power to give it a loving home, to make sure it feels welcome and safe. You do the same thing for old dolls, vintage dolls, or discarded dolls. You take time to make sure they know they are in a safe space, welcomed into your home and life.

Sometimes if you are aligned with dolls, a haunted doll may seek you out. Such an experience happened to me in New York City, while I was there for the Occult Humanities Conference in October 2023.

The Conference took place a few weeks before Halloween, Samhain, All Hallows Eve.

One evening, after the close of the day's events for the conference, myself and a few of my fellow colleagues decided to walk through the city in search of pizza. New York is famous for its pizza, and one of my buddies knew a really good place within walking distance. It was a beautiful night, so off we went in search of the pizza restaurant.

We passed lots of brownstones and stores decorated for the season. It was truly magical. We sauntered down a tree-lined street, lit by glowing antique streetlamps, my friends were a few steps ahead of me. I tend to walk slow. I'll get there, but it may take me a bit a longer to arrive, as my legs and feet aren't what they used to be, now being in my 60s. That's okay. Perhaps walking slower gives me an opportunity to notice things that are magical and appreciate the beauty of the rarely seen. As I am naturally inclined to notice and feel the presence of the quiet whispers of the unseen, having to slow down at my age is an enhancement to my life.

As we continued to walk down the street, feeling the promise of delicious New York pizza, I noticed a doll in a window. The shop was shut, but an eerie light was cast upon her. She had obviously been placed there for the season, but I was drawn to her in a way I can't explain. She was the height of a small child, and I believe she had a teddy bear dragging from one hand. A cool blue light shone upon her through the basement window at the bottom of black wrought-iron stairs.

She looked at me. I felt it.

Of course, it was dark. It was now nighttime. Everyone was hungry and focused on getting to the pizza shop.

No one saw her or took notice of her, except me. And to this day, I still keep thinking about that doll.

Was she haunted? Maybe. Did she need me to rescue her from that shop? Perhaps. Or maybe something between us clicked. It was a moment. But I know that doll felt me, and I felt her. I just hope wherever she went after I saw her, she's in a good place.

Do Dolls Have Spiritual Value?

I think my stance on the question of the spiritual value of dolls is clear. The title of this book, after all, is *The Spiritual Magic of Dolls.*

Through these pages we find our way exploring the ideas of dolls being haunted, scary dolls, scary movies featuring dolls, the history of dolls, and you will also meet three of my dolls who stay by my side, giving me their attention and inspiration.

Today, as I write this chapter, the weather has finally become overcast and cooler. We're in a break from the hot, hot summer weather, the summer weather waning, and I, for one, am truly happy about it. Living in Denver, Colorado, we're blessed to have the four seasons, even though you can find snow any day of the year if you go up to higher elevations. As the summers have progressively gotten hotter and hotter, I have become more of a winter person. I look forward to cool mornings and chilly nights. I look forward to yard work ending as plants and trees enter their dormant stage. And even though I am not a skier (although I do lodge life very well) I look forward to the snow. Colorado has some of the most beautiful snow in the world. It sparkles.

Perhaps the sparkle we see in the crystal bright, fresh Colorado snow is the same spiritual sparkle you get when gazing at a doll who has become meaningful to you.

When you look lovingly at your dolls, they lovingly return the gaze. It is a *spiritual* feeling. You may not be able to exactly explain what that feeling is, but you know *it*. The doll is returning your affection.

Sometimes they smile at you without you activating the engagement. Many times, you can simply look at your doll and they are smiling at you. I love that! And sometimes the more you look at them, the more they seem to smile. I truly believe my doll-loving people *know exactly* what I'm talking about!

I am a spiritual, magical person. I feel deeply. I am highly intuitive, and deeply attuned to nature and the rhythms of the Universe. I am a highly sentient being. I know I am not alone in these feelings or experiences, and I believe many people who find kinship with dolls may also experience the world in this way.

Our dolls sit quietly, absorbing the energies of life. They bear silent witness to our feelings and emotions. They mark time by their age. They can exist long after our human lives are gone, which is why dolls have a presence. They inhabit our personal spaces then move on to new spaces or places, long after we have gone. They carry those experiences and journeys with them.

The longer a doll is around, the more spiritual they become, just like us. If we open to the magic of things that we may not quite understand but know in our hearts there is meaning for us, we also grow more spiritual. Our dolls can become our companions on the journeys of our lives. They love to go on trips. They like to travel and be passed on to loved ones, families, and friends. They appreciate being considered and recognized as heirlooms. Yes, dolls have spiritual value.

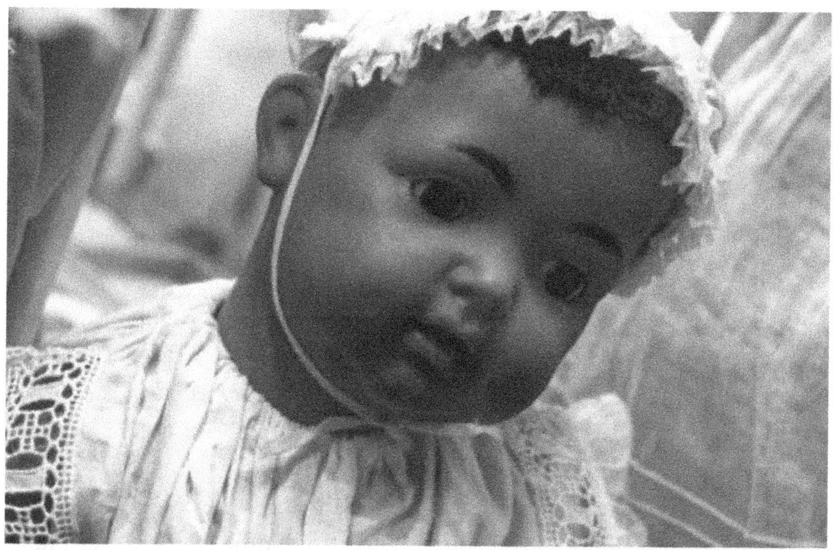

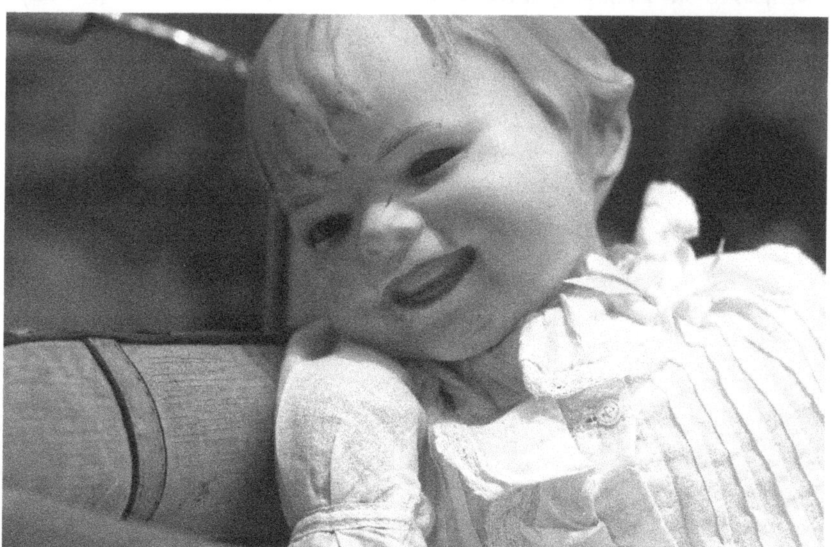

Dolls have a quiet presence, yet they speak to us..

A doll's value changes over time. In my home we are big fans of the *Antique Roadshow.* I love it when dolls make an appearance on the show, and they evaluate the worth of the doll. It is exciting that folk dolls are now gaining in value. Many higher valued dolls come from homes or families who acquired them through inheritance, or the doll was purchased from a European country long ago.

But no one can truly put a monetary value on a doll. Yes, it is wonderful to hear your doll may be worth hundreds of dollars, but does that really matter to you?

I would venture to say the *true value* of your doll is how much you love it, what it gives to you when you hold it, gaze upon it, hug it, sleep with it, carry it with you when you move or travel, or when you lovingly give it to someone else. A doll's true value is measured in *love.*

A History of Dolls

We know dolls are magical. Being created in the image of human beings gives them an eerie, mystical, and some may even say, a chthonic quality. And while the chapters of this book focus on the otherworldly quality of dolls, we must also focus on the nature of dolls as collectible items, one with a long history. This history is rooted in their ability to become valued, antique items sold at auction houses and websites.

As I combed through hundreds of pages of text in books written for doll collectors, I found the history of collecting dolls and how dolls are named and categorized to be enlightening and disturbing. Many words and descriptions of dolls listed in books for collectors made my skin crawl, and yet it filled me with deep conviction for dolls that call to me.

On many occasions I have been drawn to a little Black cloth or porcelain doll in a store, simply because I know the image she was created

in, to reflect, is not one of positivity or joy. Time and time again I came across horrible words such as "Pickaninny" or "Topsy" listed in doll collector books, used to describe these dolls. These names are abhorrent to me. They stir powerful imagery related to the phrase "beauty is in the eye of the beholder." Dolls categorized by these names, evoke painful feelings of how Black children can be viewed or portrayed when seen through a certain lens, associated with our hair, our skin tone, and what is perceived to be beautiful. It causes a deep pain in my soul. Case in point; I love movies. I love watching old movies, movies from the bygone era of old Hollywood. I am a fan of musicals, and especially movies shot in Technicolor, which look like you're inside a beautiful art deco building, as you watch them from the comfort of your living room. During the writing of this book, I was doing one of my favorite things, which is to watch old Hollywood movies on a Sunday. For me, watching movies provides a form of escapism I truly enjoy. I love to settle in, turn the lights down low, light candles, snack on my favorites snacks, and allow my mind to meld with the cinematic story.

On this particular Sunday movie watching day, I was enchanted, enthralled with a movie I had never seen, *Lullaby of Broadway,* released in 1951, starring Doris Day, who is one of my old-time favorite movie stars. I was super happy watching this film, because it showed off Doris Day's prowess as a dancer, something you don't readily see in her later films. As I sat with my eyes glued to the screen and my mouth hanging open, during one particular fanciful, dance scene, where the movie is portraying famous dancing dolls on stage, I noticed in the background, a theatrical shelf, made to look as if it was shelving for all types of dolls, while the stage performance of a magical doll took place. And to my horror, I saw not one, but two dolls portrayed as Black "pickaninny" or "Aunt Jemima" dolls. My heart sank. Here during this wonderful scene that was captivating my imagination were two Black dolls in the

background, with grotesque features, their hair tied up in rags and pigtails, and terribly painted, enormous lips that were several sizes too big for the faces. There were also dolls resembling clowns on the theatrical backdrop.

Granted, this backdrop was only on screen for a moment, but in that moment I was jolted out of the magic and into the reality of how little Black dolls used to be so readily portrayed. I then found myself literally holding my breath, hoping that this movie, the Sunday movie day experience I was so thoroughly enjoying, would not further sink into the abyss, and have performers appear in "black face." Thankfully, that never happened, and I was able "to do the work," which means compartmentalizing what I had seen in order to return to my magical, movie place of enjoyment, but it wasn't quite the same as before I saw the Black dolls on the backdrop in the movie. As much as I enjoyed *Lullaby of Broadway,* it will now always have a bittersweet moment for me. If I ever watch it again, I'll just look away when that scene appears, because I cannot change the past, cinematic history, but I can choose to look away. And this is why I used to want to buy up all the little Black dolls I would see in stores, who were made in this manner.

I also came to learn that, if you are approaching dolls from purely a collector's viewpoint, you would use these names, such as "pickaninny, topsy, and Aunt Jemima," and then most likely add a disclaimer. It is my hope collectors would pause and think before using these descriptive, ugly names to characterize Black dolls of this nature.

As I continued my research, I learned dolls made in the image of European ancestry, especially those with Bisque heads and white, porcelain skin, fetch quite a high value on the market.

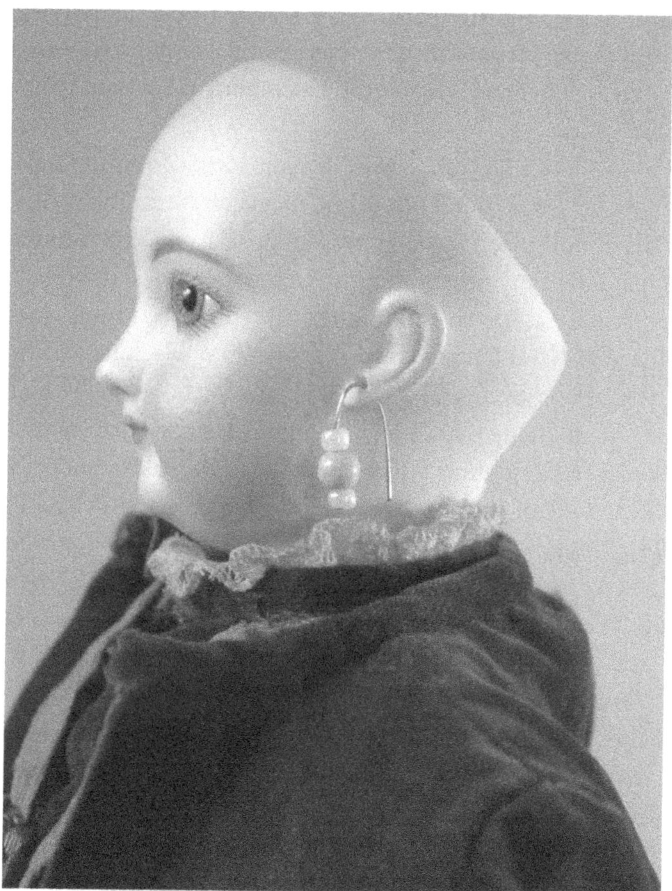

Bisque heads, white porcelain skin, and European details have historically been "valued."

However, it is encouraging to see with the passage of time that dolls whose images reflect Ethnic images from their cultures—such as Black/African American dolls, Native American dolls, and dolls from countries in South America, just to name a few—are now highly sought after collectibles.

Seminole dolls, 1895-1905.

Words are powerful. Reading the descriptions of non-European dolls in books intended for collectors was hard on my heart. Yet we persevere. At times, to heal our wounds, we must take the long view, and hope that as time continues to evolve, dolls who were once seen as offensive and not worthy of value, will become actually the opposite, and collectors and manufacturers of dolls will come to realize that representing the cultures of the world through the images of dolls is indeed a worthy, necessary, and important venture.

My collection of Black dolls is highly precious to me. I have several Black dolls which fit the category of "collectible." Some are approaching the designation of "antique," which is used to identify any doll over seventy-five years old.

I intend to hold onto my collection, not only for monetary value, but because their historical and emotional value is priceless, especially viewed through the lens of how collectors prioritized European dolls in earlier decades. As I continued my research, working my way through books designed for collectors, it made my stomach turn to see photos of dolls created in images I personally find offensive, as well as their given names. However, as earlier stated, dolls reflect the time and the history of the age from where and who made them.

We can re-parent and re-home dolls which may have been created in an image not pleasing to us. We cannot change the past, but we can move forward, enlightened and determined to create a new future.

As I continued to turn through the pages of research material designed for collectors, I was very excited to find a photo and a description for one of my re-homed dolls!

In *The Art of Dolls 1700–1940* by Madeline Osborne Merrill, on page 344, there was the description and photo of my doll. The description cited words such as "inexpensive" and "tufts" of hair.

It was exactly for this reason that I was drawn to this little Black baby doll. Her hair looks like a hot mess (as per my research, I now know her hair style is in the style of the three pigtails, worn by pickaninny dolls), she is wearing a raggedly cotton diaper, and her painted eyes stare vacantly outward, asking for a home. Her tufts of hair were barely attached, and she was very dusty, sitting on the shelf in the antique store where I found her.

Of course, she called to me, and I brought her home! She came into my doll family from my heart. As such her value is priceless to me. She now sits upon a tufted throne of a doll chair, upholstered in the deep, regal, and royal color of red.

It matters not she was listed as "inexpensive" in the collectors' book. However, finding her listing was quite the surprise. I had no idea of her material legacy!

My sweet little Black baby doll.

As a magical person, you too may have dolls that fall into the "collector" category, as the doll industry is mighty and vast. Several organizations, societies, and websites exist for the preservation and the determination of value for dolls. You may never wish to sell your dolls, but it is good information to know how dolls are catalogued and valued. However, no one can put a price on the magical value of your doll. That evaluation is one determined by the love and relationship you have with your dolls.

What if Dolls Aren't for Me?

Many books, movies, stories, and articles about dolls focus on the fear of them. They are immersed in the dark and scary atmosphere, surrounded by tales of haunted dolls, or even demonic experiences attached to dolls. If that was not enough, they seek to turn the reader's lens upon frightful places, describing how to use "Voodoo" dolls or poppets intended to cause harm by crafting dolls from fabric, clay, or wax.

Of course, many of these tales fall into the category of fiction. But we know the best fiction carries a grain of truth. Many a writer immerses themselves in tales of the occult, the paranormal, and the supernatural. The scarier the words, the better. Fear sells. And some of us love a good scare. But scary is subjective, as is gore and violence, or combinations of the two. There are many levels of scary, violent, and gory. I tend to shrink away from gore and gratuitous violence. Everyone has their own levels of comfort, and what they can and cannot unsee. I have also found highly sensitive, intuitive, and empathic people are more cautious around what they view or read.

As I write these words, the first day of October has finally dawned. My social media is already ripe with scary pictures of dolls. There is a plethora of videos, reels, and posts that feature frightening images of dolls. Yes, October is the season of the Witch, and being scared out of your wits can be fun, if you like that type of thrill. Dolls do possess the ability to be scary. But they can also be comforting and loving.

This book, my dear readers, is crafted and written for the magical practitioner, witch, or for a person who has a love for dolls and would like to learn how to bring them comfortably and lovingly into a working and familial relationship. This book seeks to connect those who love dolls or are drawn to dolls, especially dolls that may have had a hard life before they ended up coming into the lives of the reader.

Many people have dolls they don't understand or can't seem to discard, yet they don't know what to do with them. They find themselves caught in the paradox of "this doll creeps me out, but I can't get rid of it!" These people approach me at conferences, speaking in low voices telling me about dolls they were gifted or have inherited and aren't quite sure what to with a doll, or how to handle the doll.

The Universe works in mysterious ways.

My heart goes out to these people. I can see on their faces they are conflicted about the doll or dolls, and how to let go or move the doll on to a better place. They also have deep feelings if they know the doll isn't one *anyone* should handle, should they even consider passing the doll unto another person?

As I continued to work on the pages of this book, I found myself in a similar situation.

I was driving home from an appointment on a sunny spring day, after having a wonderful pedicure (it's so lovely to get your toes done!). I was in a very relaxed, calm state of mind as I drove my car through a plush tree-lined neighborhood, when I saw through my car window a little white doll lying in the street! I thought I was seeing things. Did I really see a white baby doll lying in street?

I had to drive down a few blocks to turn around and confirm what I had seen, due to construction in the area. But sure enough, after parking my car, and walking a short way, I came upon the baby doll lying in the street.

I paused and looked around. Normally this neighborhood is filled with walkers, parents and kids, dogs and strollers. But on this day, there was absolutely no one around except for me standing with my mouth open, staring at this baby doll lying in the street. There was an eerie emotion swirling around the blackness of the shiny asphalt, and the doll all alone in the street.

The "baby," found abandoned in the street.

It struck me as odd nothing else was with the doll. There was no stroller, no blankets, no toys. Just the doll lying face up, alone in her jammies. That was it. Her big blue eyes were open, staring at the sky. My heart felt a tinge and a pull. I will share most of my doll collection consists of black dolls, and that reflection gave me pause in my thoughts as to whether I should bring this doll home with me. I wasn't sure she would be a fit with my doll family. However, I had recently added to my doll family a little white doll, who is of a special nature, so it's not as if my doll family isn't accepting and inclusive, but this doll baby was different. She's a *baby.* But I already knew in my heart, when I saw her lying in the street from my car window, there was no way I was going to abandon her.

As I looked around, I noticed a large tree next to a lovely, manicured home with a verdant curbside, close to where the doll lay, but it didn't feel right for me to place the doll on their property. So I picked the doll up and gave her a good looking over. Poor thing, she had asphalt marks on the back of her clothes! Did someone just chuck this little doll out the window and keep going?

I couldn't just leave her. Instantly, in that moment, after picking her up, turning her over and looking at her clothes, I made the decision that she was coming home with me. I cradled her and tenderly placed her in the passenger seat of my car, and talked to her for a while. She seemed to be in a state of shock. I told her about my doll family and assured her she could stay with us for a while. At the time I wasn't sure she would become a family member. I don't have many baby dolls, and, to my surprise, I discovered once I got her home that she is huge compared to my other dolls! She is the size of a real human baby and is larger than most of my other dolls. She is a big baby.

Now that I have learned how to identify dolls through my research, I looked for a tag or a mark on the back of her neck. I found a tag attached to her lower body which identified her as an Adora doll. I went to the *adora.com* website and learned all about her. What a sweet doll! These are award winning dolls made to inspire play in children! But that still didn't answer the question: why was she lying in the street?

During an Instagram reel dive, I had laughed myself silly watching videos about siblings who aren't too happy when a new baby comes into the family. Was this the fate of my doll? Did a sibling receive her and was none too happy about the gift? Was it an older brother or sister who had chucked her out of the window? Did she secretly get turned out of her stroller by a jealous sibling? I had no idea. I posted a picture of the doll on my Instagram, but no one claimed her.

And this is where I found myself in a conundrum. It was not truly my intention to keep the doll. I began to wonder if I had entered into my first

"foster home" situation for dolls who need a place to live, until they find their true home. But as days and weeks passed, a connection developed between me and this big baby doll I had found in the street. My other dollies also accepted her, although they did give her a side eye or two at her gigantic size. I am happy it worked out. She has chosen to stay, and we have *chosen* her to stay with us. She has given me the experience of hugging and caring for human size baby doll. And I feel good knowing I rescued her from the street. Our connection is secure.

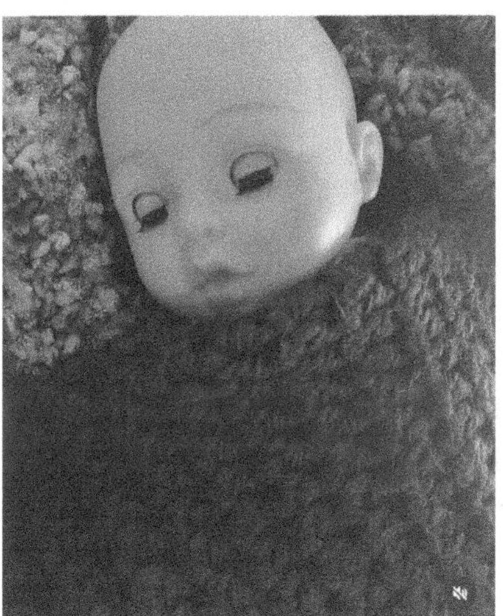

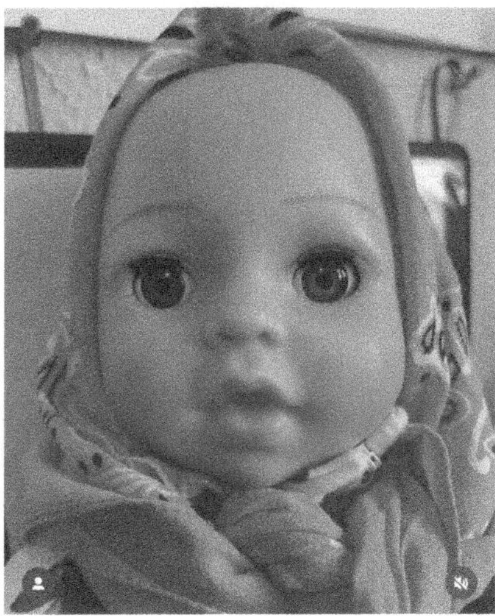

The "baby" spent some time in recuperation (left) and is now healthy and smiling (right).

Spiritual and magical people understand spiritual connections. They understand there is a powerful presence *connected to all things. They know how one chooses* to use that power is a choice each magical practitioner, or witch needs to make, hopefully in accordance with the blessings of their higher power.

Although I have shared my experience of finding and keeping my doll I came across in the street, I know you may want to know my suggestions for letting go of a doll you may feel should not be passed on to anyone.

It is a sad day for me when I come across these stories, and I see the anguish on people's faces who feel they have a doll of this nature. I feel sad for the doll and the person. It is a time of grief. The doll must be returned to the earth.

All dolls are creations made from materials from Mother Earth. Nothing we wear or use for our daily lives comes from anywhere else, other than the Earth, herself. It is her body from which we rise, and unto her body we return at the end of our lives.

If you find yourself in this situation with a doll you feel you can no longer keep, but also do not wish to pass on, or gift to anyone else, the best thing you can do is return the doll to the earth. Let our great Mother Earth receive your doll. I also suggest keeping the burial place secret, leaving no marker or stone. However, if you feel you must tell someone, be sure that person is a trusted confidant.

How you choose to bury the doll is completely up to you. If you had a loving relationship with the doll before you decide it must be buried, I suggest having a funeral or service for it, in the manner you would lay a loved one to rest. Funerals and services for the Dead are extremely personal affairs, so I give people autonomy on how best to proceed in those areas. As a magical person I might include herbs of lavender, rosemary, sage, and sprinkle some Florida Water upon the doll before I cover it with earth.

If there has never been a loving relationship between you and the doll, and you decide it is time to bury it in the ground, I would suggest covering it completely with salt, pulverized camphor, and dragon's blood resin. You can find camphor and dragon's blood resin at metaphysical shops and online retailers. I suggest not burying the doll in your backyard or anywhere near your home. You may need to take some time to scope

out a place for the ritual. Once you bury the doll, when you are done with the ceremony, don't look back. Not looking back is an act of trust between you and Spirit. Trust in your Higher Power and/or Deities to watch over your work. Go home via a different route. Be sure to wash your clothes and say a prayer or words of affirmation for blessing and protection. Relax in the knowledge you have your done your best to send the doll on its way. It is no longer your responsibility or concern. Allow Nature and Mother Earth to receive what you have given back to it.

While I feel the need is important to address how to let go of a doll you feel is causing havoc or untoward emotions in your life, this book is not written to flame the fears many people have of dolls.

My sincere hope is these words will be a helpful guide to people who find themselves drawn to dolls, and want to be closer to them in magical, loving ways. You may be that person. You may want to become that person. You may also be the person who in no way wants to have anything to do with dolls, no matter how they come into your life, which is totally okay! Your interest in dolls might be nothing more than an intellectual curiosity. However, if you've picked up my book, and are reading these words, I have a suspicion, you may be willing to explore how to build a closer relationship with dolls.

CHAPTER TWO

Spiritual Magic: Working with Dolls

Meet My Dollies!

My first doll I'd like to introduce you to I found in a bin in an old decrepit store that sold vintage furniture. She's the oldest, in family order, of the dolls I am introducing to you through the pages of this book. She is our cover doll! I will say, she is very happy and pleased to be on the cover of this book. She has caught the attention of doll lovers and magical people everywhere. She is representin'!

I remember that the store I found her in was massive. My hubby and I used to love to wander through it, taking our time, never knowing what we might find. Far away, tucked in the back of the store, in a room that felt more like a garage than a showroom, we came upon a wooden playpen full of dolls. I recall the large room was not well lit, except for the sunlight that poured in through gaps in the ceiling, and a few industrial lights haphazardly strung across the center. It was also chilly in the room.

My first doll, Shindana.

I couldn't see or feel any heat in the area. In short order, the massive room was filled with long dusty tables and pieces and bits of junk that even a savvy shopper would be hard pressed to classify as treasure.

At first sight, when my eyes landed on the playpen stuffed to the brim with dolls, I was shocked. I couldn't believe there were so many dolls seemingly all hanging out together in such a haphazard fashion. Some dolls were upside down, and some had their legs and arms sticking through the slats in the playpen. Some of their clothes were dirty, tattered, and torn. It was obvious that not much love or consideration had been given to their care. A lot of the dolls had matted hair and disheveled clothing. It made me sad to see so many dolls in such a state.

As I looked carefully at the dolls, picking up one, moving others aside, I saw her. There she was stuck in the corner of the shabby playpen, down towards the bottom with all the other discarded and unwanted dolls. My heart leaped upon seeing her. I had to have her. I fished her out, purchased her, and brought her home with me.

She has strange eyes. That's what drew me to her. Her hair is wild, which I've never combed, and she's never really had any clothes. She came out of the playpen this way. Naked, her hair a hot mess, with her beautiful amber eyes. I love her brown skin, her wildness. Her hair and her brazenness are one of her superpowers. I would never force any ridiculous standards of societal beauty upon her.

When I look into her gorgeous amber eyes, it is hard to tell if she is looking at me. Is she looking at you, is she looking at both of us at the same time, or what exactly does she see? She's friendly, to me, but I wouldn't cross her. She deserves love and respect. People who have met her in person say she freaks them out, or they find her unsettling. Ya think?! Though she has never really had any "clothes," in a formal sense, she was amenable to me covering her up with a fabulous black scarf, and she loves wearing the little witch hat, which I actually made for myself many years ago.

In the process of researching the history of dolls, I ordered a few books. They are massive tomes that have taken me into a new world about dolls, educating me about those who collect dolls and those who sell them. Dolls are special and precious—many people belong to collector's clubs, federations, and attend functions that celebrate the history and legacy of dolls.

Per my research, I learned how to identify marks on a doll which give you the history of their origin.

I decided I would look for markings on my magickal dolls, which are special and precious to me. One day I turned my doll over and looked under her hair. Stamped on her body were the words:

© 1969
SHINDANA TOYS
DIV. OF OPERATION
BOOTSTRAP INC. U.S.A.

I was shocked. My doll who I rescued from the cold, hard playpen, in the chilly, dusty vintage store, is at the time of this writing, fifty-six years old! Fifty-six!

I was absolutely stunned when I found these markings on my doll, my Black doll, whose photo graces these pages and is the cover doll of this book. My beloved doll with her strange eyes and wild hair, who came to me more than a decade ago, who was considered discarded, stuck way down in a corner, in a bin, in a vintage furniture store.

The store where I found her closed years ago. The building remains but it has been refurbished and houses a new business. Finding my doll is another example and twist of fate of letting my intuition guide me. It is highly possible the store could have closed without me ever setting foot in it and finding my doll. For years, we drove by the building in its incarnation as a collectible store without stopping in to shop. It was only a

handful of times we parked and took a look around at the mountains of stuff for sale.

Had I not had the passion to write this book and learned about markings on dolls, it is also highly possible I may have never discovered her true origin story. I simply loved her for who she is. You can imagine my delight the day I turned her over, looked under her hair, and I discovered she is a Shindana Doll, made in 1969! I still get emotional when I think about it. This is another example of following my gift which connects me, and helps me understand and listen to dolls.

I learned she was made in Los Angeles, California, by the Shindana Toy Company, founded after the Watts Riots in 1965. Shindana is a Swahili word which means "compete."

Further research led me to *pbssocal.org* where I watched an amazing video titled "Lost LA: Shindana Toy Company: Changing the American Doll Industry."

I highly recommend watching this video. The video does a tremendous job in conveying important knowledge regarding the creation and the founders of Operation Bootstrap and Shindana Toy Company.

The founders of the company made dolls for Black children so they could see themselves represented in a positive light, and inspire the desire of self-love, achievement, and the knowledge and power that we can be and do anything! I too felt empowered when I pulled my doll from the playpen and brought her home with me.

The real goosebumps and shivers came to me when I realized I was living in Los Angeles in 1969. In 1969, I was nine years old. I can recall family trips and school trips to Watts, to see the neighborhood where the riots had occurred, and also to visit the famous Watts Towers.

But the real question is how did my doll go from being in Los Angeles, CA, in 1969, to me finding her in a bin, in vintage furniture store in Denver, CO?

It's mind-boggling. It's magic. It defies logical explanations.

I've lived in Colorado continuously for more than forty years. I lived in Colorado Springs and Boulder, before finally moving to Denver in 1985. If memory serves me correctly it may have been the year 2014 when I found her. Or did she find me? Did she save me, or did we save each other?

I know I was immediately drawn to her. I knew she was special, and she needed to be rescued from that horrid bin of dolls. Obviously, whoever put her in that bin had no idea of her history or worth. She was cast aside, along with all the other dolls no one felt were special. I knew I needed to bring her home and bring her into my family. But until I began to work on this book, I didn't know her origin story. Now her story is complete. Which is why I've never re-touched her hair, although she is resplendent in her little witch hat. Hat or no hat, she is enough. She's existed for fifty-six years, and hopefully she will be around for many more years.

She has imbued me with her magic ever since I brought her home, which is also why she made the leap from simply being magical to magickal. She carries secrets and whispers to me. I understand her. I get her. She and I are connected on many levels.

Her discovery story is an example of why dolls are powerful and important, especially to magical, intuitive, empathic and sensitive people, children and adults. They keep telling us stories and help us piece together parts of our own lives that may be buried or forgotten for years. And in the uncovering and re-discovering of those memories, we may find a deeper and more powerful magic awaits us.

• • •

My second doll I'd like to introduce to you to came into our family from the city of New Orleans. As hubby and I were strolling down Magazine Street on a glorious autumn day, we came across a vintage antiques and collectibles store, which caught our attention. Naturally we went inside.

New Orleans is a city full of heirlooms, hidden treasures, antiques and magical items you won't find anywhere else in the country. It is a shopper's delight. A place where you may find that one item that will make your dreams come true. As you stroll along lost in the mystical world of the Big Easy, it is easy to forget something great may be waiting for you behind a dusty window or sitting quietly on a shelf. Part of the joy of visiting New Orleans is going with the flow. Shopping in New Orleans is a curio and curiosity seeker's delight.

I've found that many stores in the French Quarter, with the exception of a select few, cater to tourists. As you take time to stop in one store, thinking you've found a small treasure, leave that store and pop into another, and you'll find the same item. The only difference may be the item may be displayed differently or called by a different name. Savvy shoppers beware. It's also hard to tell the real thing from a fake after you've been eating some of the most delicious food in the world and hanging out in some of most fabulous bars ever known to man. Trust me, I know! I prefer to leave the French Quarter and head up to the Garden District to do my shopping or stop in a little shop in Algiers, the historical neighborhood on the west bank of the Mississippi River, which is also a great place to visit and just a ferry ride away.

On this trip to New Orleans, upon entering the vintage and collectibles store on Magazine Street, we did our usual routine, which is that we start out together shopping, but if something catches our eye, we'll veer off and spend some time individually looking at the item, while the other keeps shopping. This is what I was doing when my husband called me to come look at something that had gotten his attention. He was nearing the store exit, and I was fascinated with some other trinket (shiny things!), hesitant to leave my aisle. But I do trust his nudging when he finds something that he wants to me to see.

She caught his eye first from her place sitting on a high shelf. My husband pointed her out to me. I looked at her, reached up, and

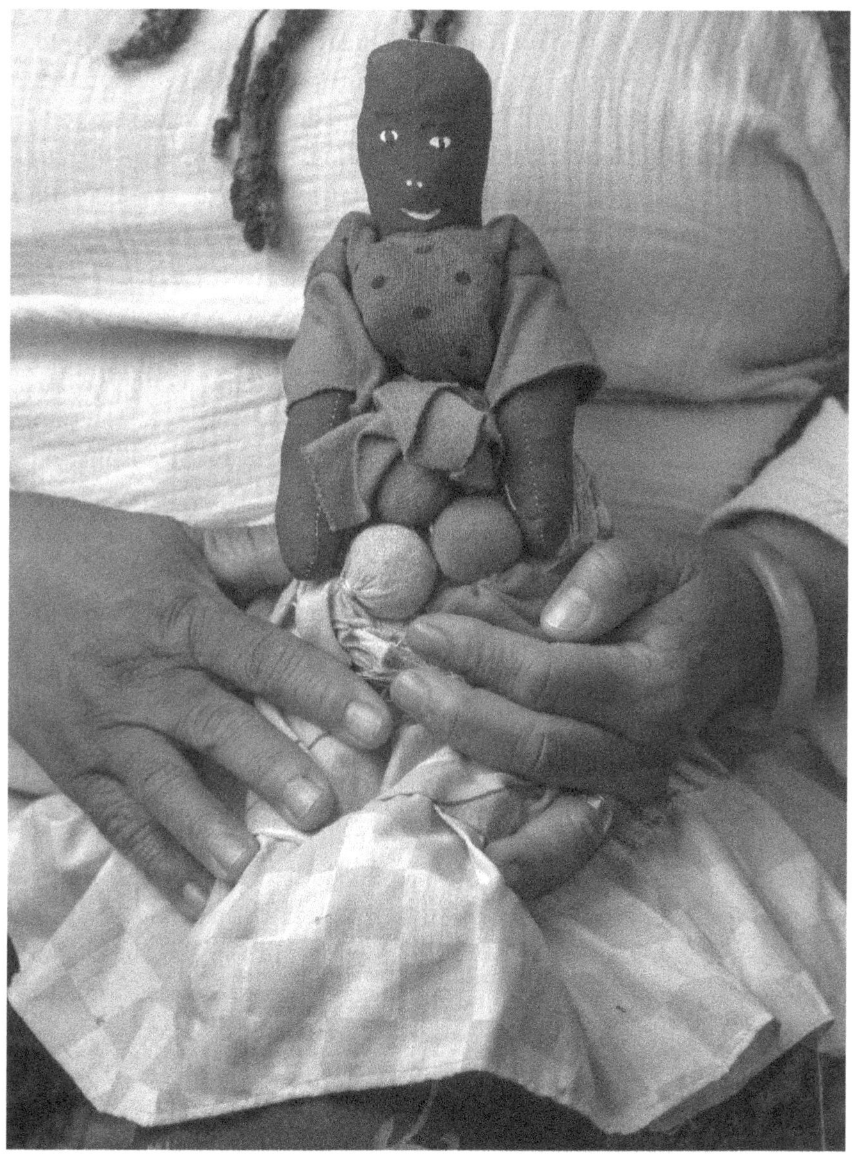

My second doll, from the Blue Bayou.

immediately took her down from the shelf. I couldn't stop staring at her. I was enchanted by her handmade body and her black face. Her painted eyes and whimsical smile kept drawing me to her. I couldn't put her down. I wasn't sure I should buy her, but the need to keep holding her was overwhelming. My soul recognized her and in that moment I made an instantaneous decision. She was coming home with me to Denver.

As we found our way to the counter to pay for her (she was the only purchase we made in the store), I was curious to see if I could learn any information about her history. I inquired of the clerk, who appeared to be an elderly Witchy woman by the clothing was she wearing, if she knew anything about my doll. She didn't know much, but she seemed to recall my doll coming from an area they call the Blue Bayou.

With the passing of time, I've come to realize perhaps I thought the clerk said, "Blue Bayou," when maybe she said, "Bayou Blue." Per Google Maps, "Bayou Blue is an unincorporated community and census-designated place in Lafourche and Terrebonne parishes, Louisiana, United States."

What I found interesting about the location is the city of Houma, located in Terrebonne Parish. This is significant to me because during one of our trips to New Orleans, we actually traveled to Houma and attended the Rougarou Fest. We had such a wonderful day trip driving to Houma and attending the festival that celebrates the legendary, mystical, infamous, mysterious Rougarou. We ate lots of good food, listened to fantastic music, and hubby got a great t-shirt showing the face of a Rougarou. According to Louisiana folklore, the fear of the Rougarou is used by parents to keep their children in line, to keep them from misbehaving!

Did my doll help provide protection to a little kid from the Rougarou? It's possible! If I was a little kid growing up in Houma, LA, I'd sure want a dollie to protect me from a werewolf-creature-dog-headed monster!

When you look closely at my doll, you can see she is holding mojos in her basket. She is carrying a red mojo, a yellow mojo, and a green mojo. If she was made years ago in the land of the Rougarou, I could certainly see why she is carrying mojos in her basket. In my spiritual, magickal practice, the color red is used for protection, the color yellow is used for safe travel, and the color green is used for prosperity. In my first book, the bestselling *Good Juju: Mojos, Rites & Practices for the Magical Soul,* I delve deep into the creation and instructions on how to make your own mojos.

I'm so glad we came upon her in the antique store on Magazine Street in New Orleans. Here was another doll patiently waiting on a shelf for someone to recognize her value and give her a loving home. One look at her and I knew she was meant for me.

When you look closely at her you can tell she is handsewn. Someone took tremendous time and care to make her clothing, attach her basket, and fill them with handmade mojos. She came with no instructions, no written documentation, so you either recognize her for who she is, or you don't. If you know, you know.

She has been in ceremony with me. She is definitely an ancestor doll. I can find no dates or maker's marks on her body. That's okay. I know every stitch and piece of fabric is meaningful. I love her hand painted eyes, and the different fabrics, her purple polka-dot blouse, her skirt made of several different swatches, including one which appears to be African, which comprise her clothing. I love the black fabric used for her face and body. I love that she also bears physical attributes similar to mine. I love her whimsical smile that never fades. She imparts a deep wisdom and affection from long ago. I'm glad she is part of my magickal family.

• • •

My third doll—well, I've never had a doll quite like this one in my collection. She is one of the last dolls to enter into our family. When I first saw her, she shook me a bit. I found her presence a bit unsettling.

My hubby and I came across her at the Oddities Expo in Colorado Springs, Colorado, in May, 2022. (We love being on these journeys together.)

When we first walked by her, I felt a strong attraction, but I didn't purchase her right away. I had to walk around the show for a while to get my bearings and get in touch with my emotions about her. As soon as I saw her, I couldn't stop thinking about her. She stirred something deep within me and touched an emotional place in my mind. I decided to walk around the expo and if she was still there when I returned to the table, I would purchase her. I needed to allow Spirit to be a guide unto me.

Her face is powerful. Her face is bloody and scarred. Her clothes and her hair are bloody, and as she ages the blood and the scars change color and deepen. Her eyes are disturbing, and it takes a while to hold her gaze.

It is her scars, her eyes, her bloody clothes and hair that draw me to her. She has been through a *lot*. She is a survivor. Maybe that's why I was drawn to her because, in her scariness, she shows herself for who she is. She doesn't force it. She makes you realize there are very scary things that can happen, seen and unseen. This is her power. She doesn't hide herself. She forces you to look at her, if you can. She embraces the dark and scary yet shines through it. She has withstood the storms of Life.

Her face elicits gasps, fear, or deep emotions from people who gaze upon her. I know, and she knows, that she casts powerful emotions upon those who chose to look at her. Which is why I had to walk around the show and allow myself time to think about bringing her home. I had to give much thought as to how I would integrate her into my family. Not only my doll family, but my human and my dog family, too. Everyone would be affected by her presence. It was helpful my husband and I saw her together, so he was already on board with my eventual decision.

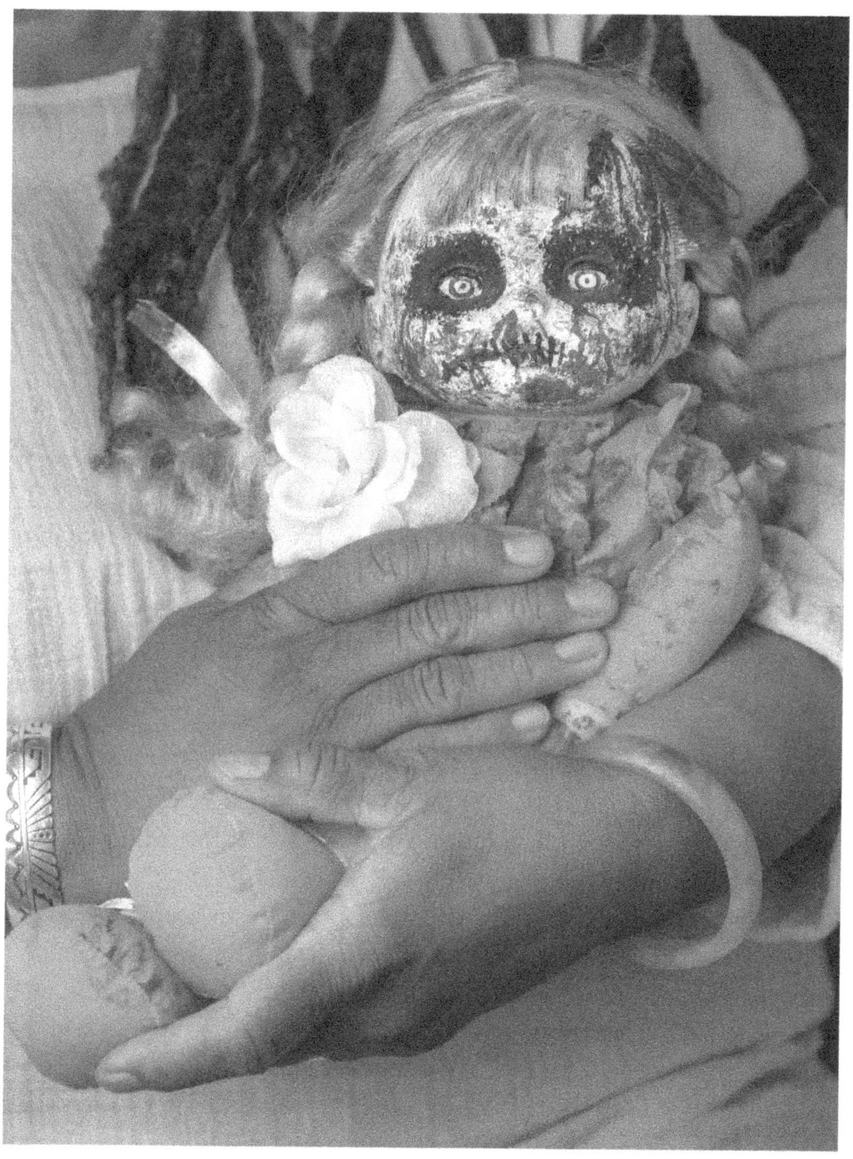

My third doll, from the Oddities Expo.

What helped me make my decision to bring her home is I know she was made to look this way on purpose.

She wasn't abandoned, cast aside, or found buried in a creepy house, or a place where maybe bad things happened. In fact, it is just the opposite. A lovely, sweet woman and her daughter, who were both present in the booth at the expo, were her creators. They both loved her. They were waiting—hoping!—that the right person would bring her home. That person was me.

A doll like this one can test you. Every doll isn't for everybody, and this doll is certainly *not a child's doll,* even though she is made in the image of a little girl. We have to use discernment about our doll purchases, or dolls that may gifted to us. We always have free will to say, "thank you but no thank you."

I will be honest, when she came home with us, we could feel her presence very strongly. I had to give her and us time to bond. I introduced to her my sweet dog, and she loved her. She sniffed her and gave her a small nudge with her nose. I knew that was a good sign.

She didn't immediately find a place with my other dolls. That also took time. They too needed space to receive her. Her presence is a powerful one, as is the presence of my other two dolls, which have become her basket mates.

I gave her time to soften and relax, and assured her she was in a safe place. As she had sat in the Oddities Expo for the entire show until I purchased her, I knew many people, as they passed her table, had cast their own feelings upon her. She evokes powerful emotions. When I brought her home, it was up to me to help her release any negativity, while also knowing and respecting her as a powerful doll. As with all acts of ritual and magick, it took some time. Finally, the energy settled, and she has become a beloved family member.

Finding a Doll

They're everywhere. You can find dolls in antique stores, estate sales, and on the toy aisle in retail stores. You can buy dolls in big-box stores and brick-and-mortar secondhand stores. You can buy them directly from "vintage" dealers, online auction houses, toy manufacturers, eBay sellers, and Etsy vendors. There is no shortage of dolls, new and used, waiting to be found, looking for a good home.

They're everywhere!

My personal favorite place to shop for dolls is at an antique store or vintage market. Sadly, there aren't as many of these stores as there used

to be. It seems online retailers have been the nail in the coffin for many mom-and-pop establishments.

When I do find a brick-and-mortar store, especially ones that sell vintage or antique items, I like to stroll the aisles with only a vague sense in mind of what I might buy. As I peruse the multitude of items for sale, enjoying the retro music that always seems to play in these stores, I hold a mental space open for a doll, for the one that catches my eye and calls me to her. I've found if I go out purposely looking for a doll, I won't find one. When you are working in the realm of spiritual magic, it is best to allow the Universe to provide. Simply holding the intention in your mind will bring you to that which you seek, and that which is seeking you.

Doll people are attuned to dolls. Doll people reach out to dolls and the dolls reach back. It's almost as if the dolls sense your doll signal vibe. In my opinion they know you are one of them. It's almost like going on a blind date. You see the doll. You wander over and pick it up. You hold it, look at it, and wait for that moment when you know this doll is for you. Lots of times that moment of recognition comes quickly. Sadly, there are times when the doll you see doesn't end up coming home with you. Sometimes after spending time with the doll in the store, you may feel the doll and you are not a fit. If and when that does happen, may I suggest gently returning the doll to the shelf with a whisper, "your family will find you." This a healing way to part from the doll, to allow moving on in search of another doll without feeling guilty that you and the doll were not a fit. It may sound crazy, but it works.

Not every doll you come across comes in shiny, pretty clothes, wrapped up in a package, never having been used. I have both types in my collection; dolls that were brand new, wrapped in boxes from their manufacturers, and dolls I found in an antique store or vintage store, sitting on a shelf, no box included, having had a life before they came to me.

I love them both. A new doll gives you the opportunity to imprint upon her your love, never having been handled by anyone else. Of course, we now know that before the "new" doll came to you that she was crafted and created by her manufacturer. Her maker or makers handled every part of her body . . . her hair, her head, her limbs, down to the very shoes she is wearing. But once she went in the box, and was ready for sale, no one else touched her until you.

I've also been blessed to receive handcrafted dolls, someone made for me. These are dolls of a different type. It touches my heart that someone thought of me as they were making the doll. These dolls come as gifts of love or appreciation. They also hold their own special places in my collection.

I have dolls that belonged to someone else previously, which lived in their homes, and when they felt it was time for the doll to move on, they gave the doll to me.

When someone gives you a doll from their heart, which previously belonged to them, it is indeed a high honor and a great responsibility. It makes me emotional when someone gifts me a doll that was previously in their family. I am honored that they know I will take good care of the doll and welcome it into my home and doll family. I'm honored to have dolls in my collection that family members felt would have a good home with me, after their dear beloved family member died. It's also a way for me to connect with friends who have crossed over. When I look at their doll, I have memories of good times we shared as friends.

When a doll that previously belonged to someone else comes into your life, and you have a relationship with the people who are gifting it to you, it is a moment of respect and honor. These dolls take time to integrate into your home and family. It's like bringing a rescue dog or cat into your home. You need patience. You need to give the doll space and allow it to adjust. You need to reassure the doll it is safe, in a safe space, and that you will take care of it. Remember the doll may have spent years, or

even decades in the home as a family member, with people to whom it too has deep attachments. Dolls also need transition time if they come to you from a previous owner. Dolls are an important part of people's lives. Their value cannot be underestimated.

I am an avid fan of the British TV show, *The Repair Shop*. When I watch *The Repair Shop* it's like having my own personal moment of Zen. The opening scenes immediately put me at ease as I watch the old barn door, which actually houses the repair shop, open. The barn sits in a meadow, which we watch change through all four seasons in the British countryside. There are ducks, birds, lush green trees, and ponds during the summer months. As the weather turns cooler, the trees change, and the craftspeople and those bringing their items in for repair, begin to wear quilted fabrics and beautiful jackets to protect them from the cold.

All of the craftspeople are masters, from the metal workers, to the doll repair ladies, to the leather repair woman, the upholstery people, the clock repairmen, and the narrator. I am always extremely touched by how the show allows people to share *their stories*. You quickly learn and appreciate the story behind the items the people bring in for repair, that really matter. It is the story of their lives, and the precious memories the items hold, that allow their lives to continue into a hopeful future, knowing their memories have been restored. Their past definitely influences their future and future generations. It really is a form of relaxation therapy, and I always appreciate there are people in the world who can repair and keep our old things alive and viable. It also makes me happy there are younger repair crafts people, beginning to appear on the show. The repair work will continue through generations. They treasure old items and know the value of old things, especially things that may have broken down from being loved so deeply. It is not a throw away and start new show. It is a "we can save it, we can restore it!" show.

My heart burst a bubble and tears rolled down my cheeks when I watched Season 6, Episode 58.

When Jess, the guest star of the episode, brings her dolls David and Amy into The Repair Shop, you can tell by looking at them they have been well-loved and cared for throughout their lives. Jess's doll David has issues with his legs. David is a little white doll, and Amy is a little Black doll. They are identical dolls, crafted to look exactly the same in appearance, except for their skin tone. It touched my heart to see the love Jess has her for dolls, regardless of their skin color. Jess tells the team at *The Repair Shop* her doll David wanted a sister, and that is when Amy came into their lives.

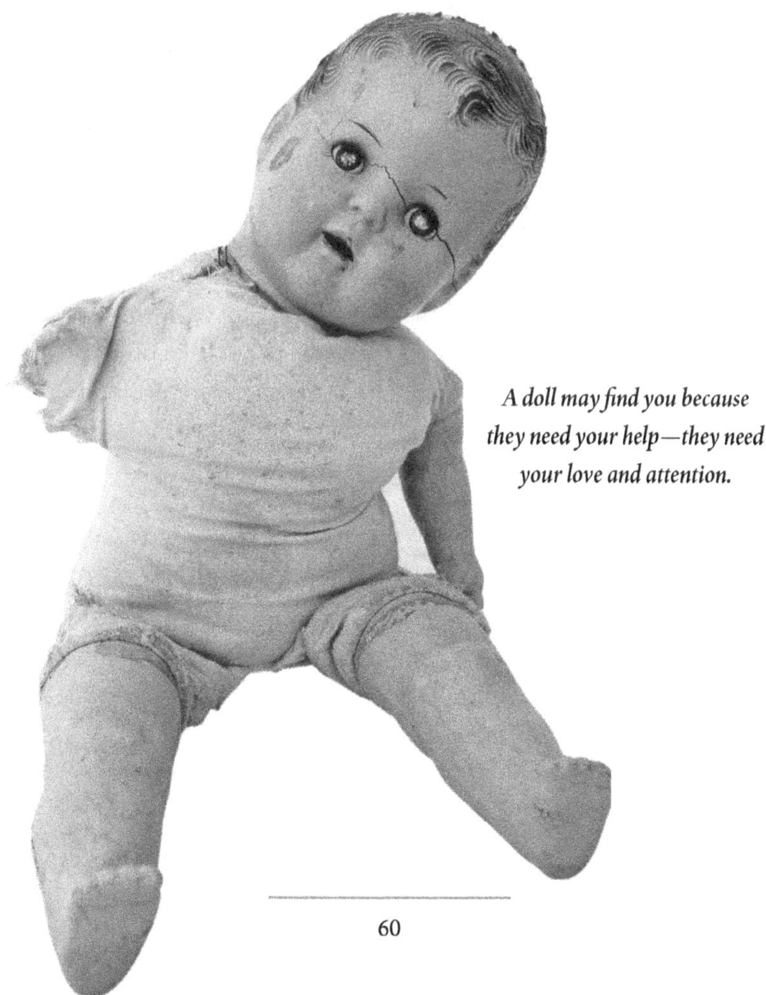

A doll may find you because they need your help—they need your love and attention.

When the dolls are revealed wearing new clothes along with a prosthetic leg created for David, you can feel ripples of emotion course through *The Repair Shop* team, Jess, and her mom. Several of *The Repair Shop* team members had wet eyes, along with me as the viewing audience, as we watched Jess look at her dolls, now repaired.

I couldn't hold back my tears. I needed more than a couple of tissues to wipe my eyes. The dolls looked beautiful, and I have never seen a doll wearing a prosthetic leg. The episode clearly showed how important it was to Jess to have her dolls repaired and returned to her. They are a huge part of her life. They matter. They are important. We love our dolls. Yes, we do.

Bringing Them Home

Unless your doll is given to you in your home, you will have to transport it from where you purchased it, or where it was given to you.

If the doll is brand new, most likely it will be sealed in a box, and bringing it home won't take too much effort. You can simply carry the doll home in its package.

However, if you are purchasing a new doll in a store, once you make your purchase, you have entered into a relationship with the doll. It matters not whether the doll is for yourself or a gift for someone dear to you. There was a moment that occurred when you looked at the doll and decided it was the one.

Handle the new doll you have purchased with care. Don't just throw the doll in the back seat with all your other purchases or shove it in a bag. The moment you purchase the doll, you are building a relationship with it. The doll *knows* you have chosen her. You especially want to handle your new doll with care if you are purchasing the doll for a child.

Why? You never know the lifespan this doll may inhabit.

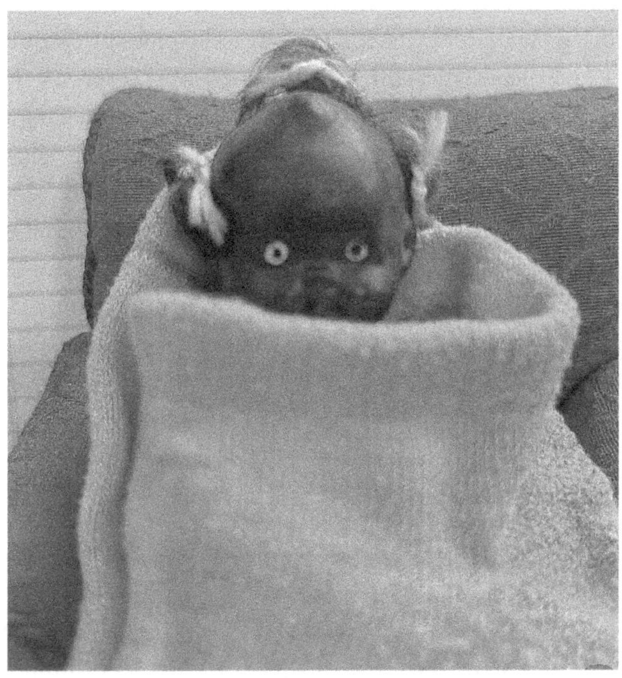

Depending upon the weather, your doll may need a blanket to keep them comfortable and warm.

This doll could be with the child from childhood to adulthood, become an heirloom, and then passed onto others. When you reach your vehicle, car, bus, or scooter, take a moment to sit the doll upright on the seat. Sit them upright either in their package, or however they came wrapped for their journey home. This small act is important in establishing a good relationship with the doll.

All dolls, whether mass manufactured or handmade, come from the vision of their creator. Somewhere, at some point in time, an artist decided your doll would look as you see her. Time and effort went into

her clothing and construction. Your doll is much more than just porcelain or fabric. She has value. Consider treating her like a piece of art. You wouldn't just shove a painting you just purchased into the back of your car. You would take time to make sure the painting was secure, that it wouldn't be damaged during transportation. Taking a moment to make sure your doll is comfortable for travel, starts the relationship off on a good foot.

If you're purchasing the doll for yourself, you also want to give it loving care.

Trust me, the doll will know if you just shoved it into the back of your car or thrust it haphazardly into your shopping bag. Have you ever sensed your dolls giving you the side-eye? And here I must speak about dolls being used as gags. I am sensitive to dolls. In the opening pages of this book, I shared how dolls call to me, speak to me. They know I *listen and see* them. Many people find humor in dolls. That's totally fine. Laughter is good for the soul. However, if you chose to use your dolls as jokes, I would suggest you ask their permission.

Be good to your dolls and they will be good to you.

Integrating Dolls into Family Life

If the doll you've decided to bring home is the first one in your collection, you will have the ease of placing her, him, or it wherever you feel they fit best. I use the word "it" because not all dolls resemble humans. There are many dolls that look like clowns, or could be beloved figures from a children's book.

I'm sure just reading the words "clown doll," may freak out many a person. Noted. If so, sorry about that! I happen to personally like clown dolls, but they must be the right type of clown. Many clown dolls are created to elicit fear. I can tell the difference between a fear-based clown doll and a clown doll that was made to bring joy. A clown doll created for children

normally will be wearing bright colored clothes and have brightly colored hair. They have joyous faces, or have painted smiles. They remind me of bubblegum balls. Demented clowns look exactly like that: *demented.* Their faces are created to intimidate. They immediately evoke a visceral feeling. But if you fear clowns, it doesn't matter whether their faces are created in joy or fear.

I don't have a fear of clowns, for which the scientific name is *coulrophobia*. When I see a clown acting evil, I feel sad for it. It has truly forgotten its purpose! Perhaps this understanding contributes to my gift of being able to communicate with dolls. (Years ago, I saw an old-fashioned trolley car going down the street with people dressed as clowns. I don't know if they were leaving an event or heading toward one, but I know seeing all of them in their clown car brought me great joy. I laughed a lot that day.)

Whether this is your second, third, or fortieth doll, great care and consideration will need to be given to where they live in your home, and with which dolls they also share a designated space.

Not all dolls belong with each other. Dolls are unique creations, even ones that have been mass produced. We don't officially know a doll's backstory when they come to us. If they have been mass produced, they could have spent months or years sitting in boxes or crates in warehouses. If you found them in a vintage store, they could have sat for hours, having people stare at them, waiting to picked up and taken to a new home. They could have been picked up, looked over, and thrown back on the shelf. A doll not wrapped and sealed and pre-made could have been anywhere before you decided to bring it home.

When you bring your doll home they become a family member, as they reside in your home with your loved ones.

Just like each family member needs their own room or a space to call their own, including our fur babies or fin babies, the same is true with dolls. In some families, children may share a room or a space, but within

that space they have a boundary to say *this is my space.* If you've ever shared a room with your siblings, you know things can go south quickly if your brother or sister crosses the boundary line in the room you share with each other!

As children get older, needs for privacy and space change. A child who once shared a room with their siblings now needs their own room. The same may happen with your dolls.

My doll dressed for the season of the Witch.

You may bring the doll home and place it on a shelf, a windowsill, or a desk you feel is the perfect place. Over time you may come to realize that space isn't working for the doll and decide to move the doll to a different place in your home. That's okay. In fact, it is a good thing if you intuitively feel the doll isn't happy in their spot and choose to move it. That's great! That shows you and the doll are communicating. You're building a relationship!

Some dolls you bring home may easily fit in with other dolls who have sat together for a long time. Some may not. Also, even though you may have love and affection for your dolls, some family members may not feel the same way about dolls. They may feel uncomfortable having dolls or even a specific doll in their space. If so, may I suggest keeping your dolls in a space where they will not experience negativity from others, and also where their presence will not adversely affect those in the house who are not keen on dolls. It may take a while to figure out the best space for the dolls that works for everyone in the household, but if you give it time, I trust you will find a solution that works well for everyone involved.

Introducing Your Dolls

I always introduce every new doll that comes into my home to my other dolls.

Dolls have feelings. They like to be seen, felt, and acknowledged. I personally have dolls that only come into the house during the season of the Witch, also known as Halloween. When I bring these seasonal dolls into my home, I too take time to re-introduce them to my dolls who live inside on a regular basis.

(My Santas are different. I love my Santas. They are Santas and not dolls in the same sense as my other dolls. Santas have and keep their own particular brand of magic. To me, Santas are secular magical creations that come from the land of the Winter Solstice. They are made with a

specific job in mind; they already have a purpose, which is to bring love, joy and happiness during the winter season, to young and old alike. But whether it is a Santa or a Halloween doll, I always get a little sad when their season is over, and they go back into storage.)

One particular doll of mine took a long time for me to find her space. She had previously belonged to someone else, and I felt a great responsibility when she was gifted to me. In addition, she is a very old doll, and I didn't want to put her anywhere that might damage her delicate clothing.

When I first brought her into my home, I placed her on my desk where I could look at her every day. I wanted to be sure I could see her and connect with her on a daily basis, but every time I opened the curtain next to my desk, I touched her thin, fabric hands, and that bothered me. I became worried I might damage her frame and clothing. I would never be able to forgive myself if after coming into my life I caused her damage! Her previous family told me she had sat on the same shelf, in the same spot for *years*. So, when she came to me, not only did I have to carry her across country, pack her in my luggage, put her on an airplane, I also had to unpack her and carry her into my home. That's a lot for a doll who lived in the same spot for decades!

I liked having her on my desk where I could plainly see her and sense how she was doing, but that spot just wasn't right. I moved her to another space in the room. She sat in that space for about a week. Nope. She didn't feel right in that space either. She kept slightly falling over which truly was a sign I hadn't found the right spot for her. No matter how hard I tried I couldn't get her to stand securely, upright. My concern continued to grow. I knew I needed to find a secure and stable spot for her to live and be comfortable in our home.

Finally, it occurred to me she would do well in a small stand. Her body is a bit fragile due to the material she is made from, and once I put her in the stand, magic! She stood up perfectly. Next, I found a space for

her on one of my bookshelves where she stands alone, in the vicinity of some of my other dolls but not with them. She needed her own space. Her own shelf. She also seems to enjoy being in a space with my books. Perhaps she lived near books in her prior home? She appears to be very happy in her new spot. We touch hands every day and I also no longer worry she'll get damaged. I know her backstory, and I want to keep her in good condition.

My dear doll from the Oddities Expo, who I introduced you to earlier, took quite a while before I could even place her in a room in my home. I had to sit with her in several different places, before I knew just where she belonged. That was a good thing. Some dolls may test you, to see if you really can handle them. Maybe you can handle the doll, maybe you can't. It won't take long for you to know if the doll is too much for you. Pay attention to your gut, your feelings, your intuition, anything that feels slightly off when you are in the presence of such a doll. If that does happen, if you feel you can't handle the doll, tell them so using kind, loving words, like you would if you were re-homing a fur baby or animal you thought would fit well with your family.

Again, as a gentle reminder, this doesn't mean your doll is "haunted." It could simply mean your doll would do better with someone else, in a different home, under their loving care.

Take your time and find somewhere or someone who you feel would be a good fit for the doll. Don't just pack the doll away and try to forget about her, him, or it. You won't be able to. The doll will sit quietly in your mind until you move it on to a better place. I know this from several conversations people have shared with me about dolls they couldn't handle or didn't wish to keep.

Also, not all dolls need to live permanently inside your home. As I have previously shared, I have dolls that come into my home as seasonal dolls, and I also have dolls who live permanently outside. The dolls who live outside like being outside. They have a role completely different from

their sisters who live inside the house on a permanent basis. If you feel your doll would be happier living outside, try finding a protected space for her and trying out the new arrangement for a few weeks. You will also need to check on your outside doll from time to time to make sure she is doing okay and that no critters or human bypassers become too inquisitive, depending upon where you have placed her.

You may find some dolls like to be seen if they are outside. Some dolls excel as "watchers." Others may like to be hidden, their whereabouts known only to you. I also find it is a good idea to routinely bless my outside dolls with sacred herbs or incense smoke. They seem to like it, and I like it too.

CHAPTER THREE

Keeping Secrets: Initiating Your Doll

A full moon shines bright in the night sky. A soft wind blows. Leaves ruffle in the trees. Something is calling to you. A whisper brushes across your cheek. Magic is in the air. It's palpable. You can *feel* it.

Time passes and a new moon is on the horizon. The heavy energy of the waning moon is lifting. You can feel the surge of a lighter, brighter, energetic time approaching. You may feel motivated to attempt reaching goals you've set for yourself. Your entire being appreciates the shift. In a few days the crescent of the new moon will appear in the sky.

Perhaps you're a person attuned to astrology, who uses zodiac time to make decisions, and you've realized now is an auspicious time to move forward with plans.

If you like to spend time outdoors in your garden, you may know the upcoming days are good for planting. Nature has sent you signals that all of the above are good times to initiate new beginnings. Your mind begins to turn to ritual, rites, and ceremony.

You've sat with your thoughts for a while. You have made a decision. You are ready to move forward in establishing a deeper connection with your dolls.

As you build relationships with your dolls through the passage of time, building trust, friendship, and camaraderie, you may decide you would like to bring your doll into the world of magick, by performing an act of initiation for your doll.

Initiation changes everything. Initiation is a step that magical practitioners often consider to be among the most life-changing events. Many people who do not follow a magical path or a path of spirituality would liken initiation to a baptism, or taking an oath in a secret society, or a sincere dedication that is performed in front of others on a similar path, or in the privacy of a sacred space where no one is present except for you and your Higher Power. It may seem strange to consider the path of initiation for your dolls. However, when you consider how personal and integral a doll can become to your life, especially as a practitioner of magical spirituality, the strangeness doesn't seem out of the ordinary. In fact, it is a very loving ritual to perform for you and your dolls.

To perform a ritual of initiation for your dolls, first choose a window of time you consider positive and enchanting. These times could coincide with the full moon, new moon, waxing crescent of the moon, the Spring Equinox, the Winter Solstice, your birthday, or times when you feel your zodiac sign is a positive relationship with the sun and moon. It could also be times when you see the first sprouts of green grass appear or you notice small flowers sprouting though cracks in the sidewalk. If you live out in rural country, you may notice certain things that appear in the natural world, that tell you magic is definitely afoot, and new beginnings are occurring.

Earlier I wrote about the difference between magic and magick. Remember that magic is about feelings and emotions. That sense of wonder and awe that is beyond your ability to describe accurately with words. You know it, you feel it, but you cannot describe it. It is a *knowing* something miraculous and wonderful is afoot. It's like the feeling you get

when you watch your favorite movie, or discover a flower growing in your yard you planted years ago that now has suddenly reappeared. Perhaps it's the feeling of finding money hidden in old purse or shoe, or maybe even a parking space after you've driven around looking for a place to park for what seemed like hours, and suddenly a space appears before your eyes. It's magic!

Magick, by comparison, is the act of using your will, words, and knowledge, in sacred relationship with your Higher Power. We use magick to bring about positive change in our lives, or the lives of others if we have received permission to act on their behalf.

Often if we work magick on behalf of others, we may be doing spell work for protection or healing. I've lit and prayed over many a candle for sick friends and family members. I've made mojos for safe travel, and I've gone to the crossroads or gone down on my knees in a cemetery seeking protection for a loved one. I've sat up for hours watching a candle I've dressed and fixed with my intentions burn, to be sure the candle burned all the way down safely. These are what I consider acts of magick. I also know when I am doing this type of work, I first spend time with my Higher Power, who for me is the Divine Mother Goddess, the power of the Divine Feminine, asking for clarity and guidance before any of the work is done. It is good to remain humble, while simultaneously acting in confidence.

Once I am done with my work, I let go, knowing I have done my best and the outcome is not up to me. I have given of myself to the best of my ability. I trust Spirit has been with me and Spirit will see my magick through to the best possible outcome.

Not all dolls are able, can be, or will wish to be part of your magickal life. Some are very happy and content just to sit in their spaces, to be gazed upon, appreciated, held, and loved. While I do have dolls that are magickal allies, most of my dolls do not occupy that role. I love waking up to my elder dolls and kissing them on their foreheads, brushing back

their hair, touching their boxes if they've never been removed from their packages, and making sure they too have made it through the night.

But some dolls have a magickal presence, and as highly intuitive, magical, aware people, we pretty much know when a doll is interested in becoming a magickal ally.

How do we know when a doll wants to do magick with us?

By paying attention.

When you are preparing to enter into a ritual space, do you get the feeling the doll is watching you? Do you feel the doll is trying to communicate with you as you prepare to honor the full moon, celebrate the seasons, or perform rituals to recognize the equinoxes? Perhaps it's just the opposite. Perhaps you've worked your magick and afterwards when you find yourself in a space with your doll or dolls, you get the feeling they are saying, "why didn't you bring us along?" The dolls are trying to communicate to you that they would like to be included. Some may think it is silly to have dolls in ritual, but they can be a source of comfort, especially if you are a solitary practitioner. Many people who practice magical spirituality spend much of their time alone, or they may live far from places where people of like-minds gather in community on a regular basis. Community and fellowship are important. Your dolls can become a part of your magickal/magical community.

I can hear you thinking, "Why would a doll need initiation to become part of my magickal family?"

By the nature of their creation, dolls are magical. They look like us. They remind us of ourselves or parts of ourselves, which is the intention of their creation. They look like babies or fancy dressed adults. They look as if they're ready to travel or gaze silently out a window, enjoying the view. They also bear silent witness to the days of our lives. Dolls can exist for long, long, periods of time. They are memory holders and keepers of secrets.

Mystical people have long employed items of comfort in their magickal workings. Some may have *familiars*, such as their dog, cat, or even a bird, who sit by them, or rest upon their shoulder, or lay in their lap, while they are in Circle or performing works of magick. A familiar not only watches, but they also give their energy to the ritual. They are an active participant in the ceremony.

A doll can be that partner for you in your magick work, if you so desire. But know approaching this work with a doll deserves time, patience, and respect. Think of your doll as a colleague, a true and trusted friend whom you love.

I am an avid journaler. I have journaled almost daily for as long as I could put pen to paper. Having conversations with our dolls can also be a form of journaling, through the act of expressing thoughts, feelings, or ideas you would never wish to share with a living soul. When you develop a relationship with your dolls in this manner, it can be a relief from trying to find secret ways to write down your private thoughts, then thinking about what to do with those words once they have been committed to paper or digital files. Also, your dolls will love that you choose to confide in them. Remember they too were created for a purpose.

With time and practice comes confidence. After initiating your dolls you may find over time, you will be able to relax as you work more and more closely with your dolls, in ritual, spell work, or ceremony.

The hardest part of initiating your doll will be keeping the work secret.

What?! What do you mean I can't tell everyone my doll is magickal?

Everything ain't for everybody.

I know we live in the age of share, share, share. Social media and algorithms can make us feel pressured to share every aspect of our lives. But some things need to be kept private, especially the act of initiating a doll. Nothing is worse than spilling your guts about your magickal work and having people disrespect it or look at you like you're crazy.

Magick is powerful. It is enchanting and alluring. Explanations are not required. People will know there is more than the eye can see when they come in contact with you and your initiated dolls.

Ritual of Initiation for Your Doll

You will need:

◊ A bottle of Florida Water (A type of spiritual cologne used for cleansings, available at online and brick-and-mortar metaphysical retailers.)

◊ A white candle

◊ A fireproof candle holder

◊ Your favorite incense: frankincense, sandalwood, or palo santo are also appropriate if you don't have a favorite.

◊ Your favorite anointing oil: olive oil works wonders if you do not have a favorite oil.

If you are allergic to any of the above fragrances, scents, or oils, you can perform the initiation with water that you have set out to charge under a full moon. I would suggest leaving the water out when you know the moon is going to be full and bringing the water in at sunrise. (If you don't know when it will be a full moon, there are many handy moon tracker apps available online.) I would caution against using water charged during an eclipse or performing this rite during an eclipse, as eclipses are known to have wonky energy. Best to wait until the sun or moon are steady in the sky.

You won't need a lot of things to initiate your doll. What I have suggested is sufficient, although you are always welcome to add your personal touches. Adding your personal touches to any ritual brings *you* into the rite. My words are simply guidelines. What is most important is

your good intentions, love, and a sincere desire to initiate your doll as a magickal creation, one that can be with you as a watcher, a protector, an ally, or participant in rituals or ceremonies.

What are the differences between these roles? A watcher keeps watch when you are performing acts of magick or are in ceremony. A protector creates a protective boundary or shield for you, regardless of whether you are physically in their presence or away from them. An ally is a good-to-go, ride-or-die magickal comrade. It knows your secrets and keeps them. A participant is just that, another active participant in your ritual.

You will need words of sincere and humble devotion to your Deity, Higher Power, or Beings—to whomever you turn for comfort, guidance and protection.

You may not wish to touch the body or clothes of the doll with oils or water. Some dolls may be very old and touching them with liquid may ruin their clothes or the material they are made from. If this is the case you can place the oils or water on your fingertips, and simply pass them over the doll, without touching it. You can also perform the ceremony and end it by blowing your breath over the doll.

Pick a time and place where you will not be disturbed. Silence your phone.

Cleanse the white candle with Florida Water by placing a few drops on your finger, then wipe the candle upwards from the middle, then downwards to the base, from the middle. Take care when anointing with Florida Water, as it is flammable. Only use a very small amount. A little dab will do ya!

Anoint the candle with your favorite oil, in the same manner as above. You may choose to say the words, "As above, so below," as you anoint the candle with your favorite oil.

Place the candle in the candleholder.

Light the flame.

Light the incense.

Hold your doll. Pass the incense over her. Lightly touch a drop of Florida Water to her hair or head. Place a drop of your anointing oil on your finger. Lightly anoint the doll's forehead. Remember that if you are concerned the Florida Water or oil may damage your doll, instead pass your fingers gently over them.

When finished, present your doll to the four directions: east, south, west and north. Raise her up to the sky. Lower her gently in the direction of the ground.

Now call upon your Higher Power or Deities to bless your doll, protect her, and watch over her. Thank your Deities and *thank your doll for being an ally unto you.*

Extinguish the flame by either pinching it or snuffing it out. If possible, allow the incense to burn safely out, as a signifier to the element of air, your work is done. Plus, allowing the fragrance to linger is a nice way to take a moment to relax and ground after your ceremony.

You may choose to have a snack or a drink when you are finished. If you do choose to have a snack or a libation after you have finished the ritual of initiating your doll, be sure to offer your doll a sip or a taste of the food as well. Just holding the libation or the snack to the lips of doll will suffice. There is no need to actually pour the libation upon the doll's lips or leave crumbs of food on the doll's body.

After putting your ritual items away and cleaning up your space, if possible, sleep with your doll or keep her next to you for the night. This will seal the ceremony.

Working with Your Doll

Initiation is heady, heavy magick. It can leave your senses reeling, your emotions unsteady, and a feeling of being disconnected from your body. If you are experiencing any of these feelings after performing an initiation ceremony for your dolls, try to imagine how your dolls may feel!

After the work is done, I highly recommend you and your doll take some time to rest. Give yourself a few nights to dream. Allow yourself time to enjoy a nice bath, or a hot, relaxing shower. You could also spend some time in nature, such as taking a stroll through a park if you are in the city, or wandering through the countryside if you live in a rural area. Any way you can find time to spend in nature after an initiation ceremony will be soothing to your mind, body, and spirit. When you return from your grounding in nature, may I also suggest allowing some down time with your dolls. Allow yourself to wander through your imagination, as you spend time holding, sitting, and being with your doll or dolls, who have now become your magickal allies and partners.

Once you are both feeling grounded (you will know you are grounded when you can hold your doll without feeling disoriented) you can now include your doll in ceremonies and rituals.

Sometimes your doll will simply bear witness to magickal works you are performing. Other times you may whisper secrets to them in the privacy of your rituals, secrets you only want them to know. You may decide your doll can hold space in a direction, or be a stand-in as an element holder. If you choose to use your doll to hold in the directions of east, south, north or west, first sit your doll in that quarter and see how it feels to you. There is no need to rush when it comes to finding which direction may be best suited for your doll. Time and practice will reveal answers to you.

If you wish to use your doll as an assistant with the elements of air, earth, fire and water, you will need to use precaution. The air element is naturally very safe. You could use a feather to wand over your doll, you could blow your breath upon your doll, or you could also simply place a non-lit stick or cone of incense near your doll.

For the element of water, I suggest placing a small bowl of water near your doll. Getting your doll wet may be detrimental to her lifespan. Many dolls, especially vintage dolls, are not made to be immersed in water.

For the element of earth, I would suggest a bowl of dirt, even potting soil will do, placed in front of your doll. If your doll is one that can be easily cleaned or brushed, I feel it would be fine to sprinkle a bit of earth upon her. Only time and trying ways of using earth with your doll will give you the answer. You might even discover your doll doesn't like being sprinkled or covered with dirt. Every doll is different.

For the element of fire, I would suggest using extreme caution. I would highly avoid any temptation to place a lit flame in front of your dolls. A good suggestion would be to light your candle (I find a tealight works best) and place the candle in a fireproof candle holder. Pass the candle, in front of your doll, making sure to stay several inches away from your doll's face. I like using tealights and tealight candle holders where the candle actually sits below the rim of the holder. Always use safety and caution when working with fire, and never leave an unattended flame near your dolls.

As time goes on, you may find yourself buying or creating ritual clothing for your dolls or gifting them with precious items for them to use in your rituals. The possibilities are limitless. You are only limited by the leaps and bounds of your imagination. You may even converse with dolls after a ritual is over to gain further insight about the ceremony. Your dolls can become your confidantes and sounding boards.

You may even wish to take your initiated doll or dolls to magical events. One great thing about dolls is you can carry them, safely tucked away in your bags, luggage, backpack or carry-on. No one will ever know they are with you, except if you decide to tell them. I've found dolls are great travel companions, especially if you are traveling alone. They welcome you when you return to your hotel room and guard the space while you're away. I like imagining the looks on the faces of hotel staff or TSA agents when they see my dolls. Fun, fun!

A few words about the relationship between your initiated and non-initiated dolls. Dolls are highly sensitive creations. They can experience the human emotions of anger, jealousy, hurt, and sadness. They may not reflect these emotions the same as a human being, but they feel them.

As I shared earlier only, a select few of my dolls have been initiated into being magickal allies. Most of my dolls are happy to occupy their doll space and have no desire to participate in ceremony or ritual, which is fine with me! It would be quite the undertaking to involve all of my dolls in ritual or ceremony. When you become attuned to dolls you will learn which ones seek to become magickal and which ones do not. But as the parent of all your dolls, be sure to appreciate and let them know they are appreciated for *who they are,* just as they are, regardless of whether they become a magickal ally or simply one of your dear doll family members. Would you like to know why so many dolls look old and sad? It is because people have forgotten they were originally created to give love and be loved. Knowing this will take you far in your relationships with dolls.

CHAPTER FOUR

Hollywood Dolls

Now that we have discussed the spiritual magic of dolls, let us turn our focus to the power of dolls in popular culture, movies, films and television.

Odds are a few dolls flashed into your mind at the mention of famous movie dolls. Both the creepy and the scary.

In the section What if Dolls Aren't for Me? (see page 36), I discussed ways to connect with your dolls that can help facilitate a relationship with them. I also discussed and shared ways to move dolls along when you no longer have a connection to them. All throughout this book so far, we have lingered on the impression people have of dolls, often considering them frightening. But I would be remiss if I didn't discuss the creepy and the scary nature of dolls.

When the weather changes and Halloween appears on the horizon, we naturally find ourselves drawn to haunting, chilling, spooky, and unsettling things. Why? Who knows? Is it because as human beings we all must face that final journey from the land of the living, and the Season of the Witch brings mesmerizing attention to those feelings and emotions? Does Halloween and the Season of the Witch make it okay to poke fun at the inevitable and our longing, gnawing obsession to

know what really does happen when we die? Do skeletons really dance and have parties?

While my dolls and I have a deep, long-lasting connection to each other, I do love the creepy and the scary. I like to decorate my home with dolls, brooms, pumpkins, candles, and paraphernalia that may give passers-by the heebie-jeebies. I tend to go with decorations that are subtle and scary, ones that hopefully make people take a second look, trying to confirm what was that they just saw? My favorite pieces are ones that move in the wind.

One of my favorite seasonal pieces of music is Bach's *Toccata and Fugue in D Minor*. I have been known to blast it through my Bluetooth speakers for all the neighborhood to hear. I actually find it soothing and comforting!

I also have my favorite Halloween movies and films, although I also watch them during other times of the year, not solely on Halloween. Here is a short list of some my favorite movies: *The Skeleton Key* (2005), *Poltergeist* (1982), *Trick or Treat* (2007), *Ghostbusters* (1984), *Ghostbusters 2* (1985), *Practical Magic* (1998), *Rosemary's Baby* (1968), *The Exorcist* (1973), *Beetlejuice* (1988), *Ghost* (1990), *Get Out* (2017), *Sleepy Hollow* (1999), and *Aliens* (1986).

There are also some Netflix series in the horror genre that have become favorites: *The Haunting of Hill House* (2018), *Archive 81* (2022), and *Dark Winds* (2022).

What I may enjoy watching during haunting season, when the moon is full, or if it's a foggy, misty, cold day, may not be some people's cup of tea. Likewise what others like can also be a "no can do," for me. What may scare you, may not be scary to me, but what scares you, could also be scary to me!

I've also learned what we may find scary changes as we age. Movies, films or events which terrified us as children may no longer give us goosebumps as adults. By the same token, as Hollywood and the entertainment

industry become more advanced with technology and the creation of new movies and films, TV shows, many new releases and October events find their way into becoming classics.

Hollywood is hypnotic. It has the power to suggest, influence, create, manifest, and inspire. Hollywood draws creatives, people seeking to be cast as actors in movies, films, documentaries, and television shows with the intention of leaving their mark on the world. Some seek Hollywood for fame and glory, while others seek Hollywood as the ultimate vehicle to express their ideas.

Hollywood also draws writers, directors, and producers. People who seek to work in Hollywood can be cast as actors, and also find opportunities on the other side of the camera, steering the direction and creation of their ideas into manifestation.

While we may logically know what we are watching isn't real, that it's just a story being told through the lens of cameras, light, action, nonetheless the best movies imprint themselves on our minds, in our consciousness, and even subconscious, if they are done in the true spirit of "*this could happen, or this might have happened.*" A truly great movie, film, or television or streaming show, can make you *suspend disbelief,* that what you're watching isn't real.

Thus is the case with dolls who have featured prominently in Hollywood productions. In this chapter we will discuss several Hollywood productions whose incredible stories have had a lasting, influential effect on the way we view the power and presence of dolls in society and popular culture.

1964: Wednesday's Doll: The Addams Family

Creator: David Levy

Writers: Seaman Jacobs, Ed James, David Levy

Air Date: 1964–1965; 64 Episodes

Main Cast: John Astin as Gomez Addams; Carolyn Jones as Morticia Addams; Lisa Loring as Wednesday Addams; Ken Weatherwax as Pugsley Addams; Jackie Coogan as Uncle Fester; Ted Cassidy as Lurch; Marie Blake as Grandmama; Thing as Itself

Awards: 1967 Photoplay Gold Medal Nominee—Favorite TV Program, Favorite Actors—John Astin and Carolyn Jones

Wednesday Addams and her doll Marie Antoinette.

One of the earliest and most influential TV sitcoms where a doll plays a supporting role is *The Addams Family*, featuring the character Wednesday, played by Lisa Loring. Wednesday's doll, Marie Antoinette, named for the famously beheaded queen, appears in Episode 1, Season 1, which aired in 1964.

Immediately we are captivated by this doll, who doesn't have a head, and is wearing the same clothes as her beloved Wednesday Addams. Although her doll has a different name and doesn't have a head, it is clear Wednesday adores her doll, who is her loving and constant companion. So profound is the story of Wednesday within *The Addams Family* series, which aired for two seasons, with a total of sixty-four episodes, that decades later in the year 2022, the powerful streaming platform Netflix revived the show, with a new spinoff title, simply called, *Wednesday*, starring Jenna Ortega.

Netflix's *Wednesday* is a smash hit. However, in this modern version, Wednesday sadly doesn't have a doll. I absorbed every episode waiting and waiting for her doll to appear. I was so disappointed when I never saw her doll!

Thing, the adorable hand-shaped character is present, but Marie Antionette has not made an appearance. I remain hopeful that, in the upcoming season, Netflix will soothe my longing, and Wednesday's doll will make an appearance! I certainly hope so, because as a fan of the original *Addams Family* sitcom, and as person for whom dolls hold a special place in her heart, it saddens me not to see Wednesday's doll in this modern retelling of *The Addams Family*. I'm sure many doll lovers and fans of the original *Addams Family* may share the same feelings.

Where has she gone? What happened to Marie Antionette? Why are we not given an explanation or backstory to the doll's location? Inquiring minds want to know. For as doll lovers, we know our dolls become more precious and valuable to us over time. We would never simply discard them. And someone such as Wednesday Addams would

never discard her doll without telling us what happened to her. Are you listening, Netflix writers?

I was fortunate to watch the original *The Addams Family* sitcom, which aired from 1964 to 1966, in real time. I watched the first episode of *The Addams Family*, aired in 1964, and thereafter in syndication, which gave me first-hand knowledge the impression that a doll with no head, who resembled her owner, can make upon a child. I also was a huge fan of the hit TV series *Dark Shadows*, which aired from 1966 to 1971, and *Bewitched*, which aired from 1964 to 1972.

These incredible television shows aired during the formative years of my childhood, and still remain the predecessors of spooky TV sitcoms. As a child I was captivated by *The Addams Family, Dark Shadows,* and *Bewitched,* even though *Dark Shadows* and *Bewitched* didn't feature dolls as part of their main storyline. Of the three shows, *Dark Shadows* was the most macabre, but I loved it. I recall having a *Dark Shadows* board game. Oh, how I wish I still had that game. What a collector's item I would have in my treasure trove of witchy curios! We know the characters from these TV shows; Samantha, Barnabas Collins, Gomez, and Morticia came into our lives through the television waves of old, yet they still remain dearly loved for their ability to be creepy and spooky, yet approachable and friendly. They are mainstays of our pop culture fascination with witches and witchcraft.

Although *The Addams Family* is classified as a comedy, it was and still is a creepy thing to see Wednesday carrying her headless doll around. Why? What happened to her dollie's head?

In my research I was happy to find *The Addams Family* available on streaming, and I watched all available thirty-four episodes. The writers packed a lot of magic into that show! No wonder its magical awe and wonder have stood the test of time and permeated the consciousness of TV lovers everywhere. The Addams family never apologizes for who they are or their beliefs. They simply are who they are, and they find humor

in the realization most people do not live their lives the way they do. It is we, the viewer and the society at large, who are out of the loop. Doesn't everyone behead their roses? I think about Morticia every time I dead-head my flowers.

The Addams family magical lives are portrayed with love. They are a tightknit family who honor their ancestors, as evidenced by the family heirlooms on display in their home and the inclusion of multi-generations of the family living under the same roof, by the presence of Uncle Fester and Grandmama, who also live with them. What magical child wouldn't want them as their cousins, grandparents, aunts, or uncles, or even neighbors who live down the street? I know I would totally accept invitations to a neighborhood BBQ (or more likely a bubbling brew) or spooky yard sale!

We first meet Wednesday and her doll in episode one, when a truant officer comes to inquire why the Addams children are not in school. The truant officer speaks to Wednesday, and gasps at her doll, seeing she doesn't have a head. Her brother, Pugsley, is offscreen building a dollhouse for his sister, while Wednesday is on her way to the cemetery to bury her doll, Marie Antionette.

What an introduction! Immediately we are taken into the world of the occult, but through the eyes of a child where everything is normal, and it is the truant officer and elementary school representing society, who are the odd ones! It is also awesome that we see no punishment issued from her parents as a consequence to her not attending school. Ah, the freedom to be a child in the home of Gomez and Morticia Addams!

Wednesday and her doll reappear in episode three, where she greets a saleswoman while sitting in the tree in front of her house with her doll. In episode ten, we learn Wednesday's middle name is Friday, as she is preparing to run away from home. She's tucked Marie Antionette into her suitcase with all her necessary items. When Gomez, her father, begins to search for her, he mentions Wednesday is a happy child, who is happy

with her collection of headless dolls, so why would she run away? In the Addams's household, a headless doll is a normal toy for a child. How lovely.

In episode twenty-two, Gomez tells Wednesday that he is going to get her a golden-haired doll. Wednesday is aghast with horror. She questions his motives. Is her father trying to punish her? Who in their right mind would want a golden-haired doll, when a headless doll is the perfect companion?! I can only the imagine the glee of little magical children everywhere who have cut the heads off their dolls, or buried them in the backyard, all cheering for Wednesday, who doesn't want "a golden-haired doll."

In Episode twenty-eight, Wednesday is seen carrying her doll upside down by the feet as she interacts with Uncle Fester. Uncle Fester is busy conjuring his latest work, which just arrived from the "Spell of the Month Club." I love it. Way back in 1965, TV was teaching us about the importance of working monthly spells. Wednesday, meanwhile, is passing through the salon, carrying her doll Marie Antionette, and talking to her invisible boyfriend, Woodrow.

Although I was only able to view thirty-four of the original sixty-four episodes through streaming, it is in episode thirty-four that Wednesday explains the reason her doll doesn't have a head. A family psychologist pays a visit to the Addams family, and Wednesday tells him she chopped off her doll's head, while making the gesture for slicing off a head with her finger. Enough said!

We also know Morticia, Wednesday's mother, had a doll named Anne Boleyn, named for King Henry VIII's second wife, who was executed by beheading. Obviously, the love of headless dolls runs in the family.

On a personal note, in 2011 we visited the Tower of London, and came upon the infamous Traitors' Gate. I loved visiting London. In fact, we were blessed to travel there again in 2017.

I had always had trepidations about visiting the Tower, as its history is filled with brutality and sorrow. Upon my visit, I steeled my courage

and forced myself to visit the dungeon exhibition. It was a chilling experience. It changed the way I used certain words that have become part of everyday vernacular.

As I walked through the Tower grounds, I dropped crumbled sage leaves on the ground. I felt it was the least I could do to offer healing and respect to the many people who were imprisoned and suffered tremendously within the tower walls.

One of the very first articles I ever had published was about Hew Draper of Brystow (today spelled as Bristol), who had been accused of sorcery and imprisoned in the Salt Tower for approximately fourteen months. Hew Draper had carved an astrological sphere, complete with symbols of the zodiac, into the tower walls where he had been imprisoned. The plaque read:

"Hew Draper of Brystow made thys spheere the 30 day of May anno 1561."

I had no idea about the story of Hew Draper or the Salt Tower when we visited the Tower of London. Hew Draper's death, or execution, was never recorded in the Tower records. We do know he left his imprint in the stone for all who visit the Salt Tower to see. Four hundred and sixty-three years later, we honor the magic and mystery of Hugh Draper. I definitely believe I was led there to honor those accused of witchcraft.

While *The Addams Family* sitcom gave us many laughs and birthed a new Netflix show based on the original television show, it also showed us the love and importance children have for their dolls. Although Wednesday doesn't have her doll in the Netflix show, in my heart I know she still has her somewhere safe. I like to imagine that, from time to time, she and Marie Antoinette have many wonderful conversations, passing secrets and telling each other stories about life as it has unfolded for them as adults. For we know our dolls never truly leave us. They remain our confidants, family, and friends for lifetimes.

1968: Barbarella: *The Motion Picture*

Director: Roger Vadim

Writers: Jean-Claude Forest, Terry Southern, Roger Vadim

Release Date: 1968

Main Cast: Jane Fonda as Barbarella; John Phillip Law as Pygar; Anita Pallenberg as the Black Queen, Great Tyrant of Sogo; Milo O'Shea as Durand Durand (the consierge)

Awards: 1970 Golden Laurel Award Nominee—Female Comedy, Jane Fonda

The movie *Barbarella* opens with a shocking scene. Jane Fonda, who plays the main character, heroine "Barbarella," proceeds to remove her space suit, showing us she is fully naked underneath. She remains naked for a large part of the opening scene. It is a shock because we don't expect her to emerge from her space suit wearing no clothes, especially when viewed in the context of 1968, the year it was released. Shortly after the shock of this scene wears off, Barbarella meets some very scary dolls! Talk about shock and awe!

In this section we focus on Hollywood movies, their influence on pop culture, doll culture, how people view dolls, and how some dolls have come to have a bad reputation. As I researched movies, films, and television shows that have greatly influenced popular culture and their portrayal of dolls, this movie stood out to me as a progenitor of doll fear in films.

The movie stands the test of time as a trippy, psychedelic adventure, even by today's standards.

Barbarella floats through time and space, on a mission to save the Universe in the name of "Love." As I watched her float naked on the screen for several seconds, I wondered if this scene was trying to make a

statement of her innocence, that she was pure love in search of a cure for evil.

As the film unfolds, it doesn't take long for her to run into a nasty group of children, in her adventure to the planet Lythion seeking the villain Durand-Durand.

One of her first encounters on the planet Lythion is with a group of children, who are all twins. These "evil" little children turn their dolls on Barbarella. The dolls are frightening. They have razor sharp, jagged teeth. They attack Barbarella, drawing blood. Barbarella does get rescued from the evil dolls, but not before her skin is bloodied and her clothes are torn!

Can you imagine the horror this scene must have caused in the audience in the year of 1968? Evil dolls, biting, ripping, drawing blood at the request of children! And not just any children, twins! Not only are the dolls evil, but so are the children. You can't trust the children or their dolls. The film also does a great job suggesting children can control their dolls and make them do very bad things.

The movie successfully taps into the innate fear that children see and live in another world, one that is not accessible to adults. Folklore is rife with stories about children who can and will do scary things. Another frightening movie to emerge during this time period is the black and white film, *Village of the Damned*, released in 1960. In this film, the children, who all look alike and have scary eyes, take over the village of Midwich, and coerce adults into behaving badly, committing horrible acts against their fellow adults. It seems the theme of children wielding evil power lies deep within our human psyche. Other movies that come to mind featuring children doing very bad things is *The Shining*—the twins in *The Shining* are legendary—and *The Exorcist*. Talk about a scary little girl! In *The Shining*, the twins (again, we have the theme of twins doing evil things) are ghosts, and in *The Exorcist*, the little girl is possessed by consummate evil.

(As an aside, I've seen both of these movies several times. They remain some of my favorite films. I tend to watch them on a yearly basis, during the winter or Halloween, Samhain, Day of the Dead, *Dia de los Muertos* season.)

To return to Barbarella, unfortunately, the dolls never reappear in the movie. However, in a later scene, *Barbarella* meets the twin girls again, and they tell her they have lots more dolls. More dolls? How many more dolls do they have and where are these dolls coming from? Who is making them on the planet Lythion, and how do the twin children come to have them and control them? It makes your blood curdle just thinking about what else may have been in store for Barbarella if she decided to play with the twins and their dolls! Maybe we need a long-awaited sequel to *Barbarella*, told from the point of view of the twin children and their dolls!

We know many people give dolls the side-eye. Many people aren't quite sure if a doll will get up and move across the room if left alone, or if it can be commanded to do harm. It's not our fault for thinking these things. Movies, television, books, and stories have done quite a number on our imaginations and minds. Who are we to say what really goes on in doll worlds?

As magical people, we know that a "presence" lives in all things, whether we believe that presence to be sentient or not. We can turn to the concept of animism, which is defined as the attribution of conscious life to objects in and phenomena of nature or to inanimate objects. We know the Universe is made up of things we cannot see or that we fail to understand, yet the Universe spins and turns, births new stars and black holes, great galaxies, and massive planets, and we have little to no understanding of how any of it takes place without any help or influence from us as human beings, whom many seem to think are all knowing and powerful. No, no, no.

I am a big fan of television shows, such as *Alone*, where people seek to stay out in the wild by themselves for an extended amount of time in an attempt to win large amounts of money, only to discover Nature is in charge, and will humble your ego in as little as twenty-four hours if you don't know how to respect or be one with the land. I especially appreciate the contestants who find awe in the animism of nature, and express wonder for the places where they attempt to make it alone.

There is a Zen meditation from Gerd Ziegler's book *Tarot Mirror of the Soul: A Handbook for the Thoth Tarot* (Weiser, 2023): "Sitting silently, doing nothing, the Spring comes, and the grass grows by itself." Our dolls definitely sit quietly, growing more precious with time and age, without any intervention from us. Yes, humility, awe, respect, and willingness to hold on to our childlike awe and imaginations, especially as we become adults, can and will carry us far. The world is full of real-life horrors, ones that don't take place on a movie screen or within the pages of a book. Just turning on the nightly news or listening to the twenty-four hour, never-ending news cycle is enough to make your blood curdle.

So when Hollywood creates a doll with razor sharp teeth that bites and draws blood at the bidding of children, it doesn't take much for our imaginations to suspend disbelief and believe that *is* possible, even if we don't consider ourselves to be magical people.

I've never seen a doll move across the floor or be in different place from where I left her at night after going to bed. But that doesn't mean when the lights go off in a room I don't look twice at my dolls. I always give them a kiss goodnight, and I greet them first thing in the morning, letting them know I see them and acknowledge them. Everybody wants and appreciates being seen and acknowledged for their contributions, and my dolls, and hopefully the dolls of many people, contribute and bring joy and happiness into the lives of their families.

My dolls have a presence of their own, and they accept, give, and receive the energy I give to them. We have a reciprocal relationship. I

give unto them, and they return love and affection unto me. The same could be said for crystals, pendulums, tarot cards, oracle cards, paintings, heirlooms, plants, gardens, your home, your dwelling . . . anything you connect to with your spiritual energy, especially over long periods of time or on a daily basis, will develop a reciprocal relationship with you.

I've never seen a doll with razor sharp teeth, but that doesn't mean one doesn't exist. I'm sure you could file the teeth on a doll, if you were so inclined, but would you want to? It's highly possible there are prop dolls from *Barbarella*, sitting in the archives of some Hollywood storage facility, or the vault of an avid collector. If you wanted your doll to have razor sharp teeth, I am assuming you would have to make the teeth out of a substance which you could attach to the doll, and then file them down. This reminds me of fake teeth people buy to look like vampires. Maybe you could convince your dentist to make some teeth for your doll, or perhaps you are friends with a talented make-up artist. Either way it sounds like a lot of work. But anything can be done once you put your mind to it.

Thus ends our time with the film *Barbarella*, the twin children and their evil dolls. Personally, after watching this film, I'm not looking to add dolls with razor sharp teeth to my collection. However, your mileage may vary.

As of this writing, IMDbPro lists that there is currently a second *Barbarella* movie in development, set to star actress Sydney Sweeney. Perhaps the dolls will make an appearance in this upcoming film. I believe they could write an entire subplot around the dolls. After all, in an alternate Universe through the magic of Hollywood, the dolls could be anywhere and do anything. Our imagination is indeed a fun and creative outlet.

1975: Trilogy of Terror: *Made-for-TV Movie*

Director: Dan Curtis

Writers: William F. Nolan, Richard Matheson

Release Date: 1975

Main Cast: Karen Black as Julie, Millicent and Therese, Amelia; Robert Burton as Chad Foster; George Gaynes as Dr. Chester Ramsey

Awards: 2019 Saturn Award Nominee—Best DVD/Blu-Ray Television Movie or Series Release; 2006 TV Land Award—Blockbuster Movie of the Week

In 1975, I was fifteen years old, living in sunny southern California. It's hard for me to believe *Trilogy of Terror* was released at the time as an ABC Movie of the Week. It scared the living crap out of me and, to this day, has cemented Karen Black as the all-time Queen of the Macabre in my pantheon of horror films I enjoy.

What was it about this film that seared the terror of dolls into our brains? The made for TV movie is actually three short vignettes, each one creepier than the last, ending with "Amelia," a short about a woman being terrorized by a fictional Zuni Warrior Fetish Doll.

The sound the doll makes as it wields its weapon, along with the sound of its tiny feet running across the floor, will forever haunt you. I know it has haunted me since 1975, yet the movie remains one of my all-time favorites. I can't get enough of it. And watching Karen Black as the only human actor in this vignette holds us spellbound. Act three is enough to warrant your attention for years. Amelia gives her all to stop the doll from killing her, only to be transformed by its magic in the end. One particular gruesome scene (for me) is when the doll bites her on her neck! Again, we have another doll portrayed in film with razor-sharp

pointy teeth. A hint to the wise is sufficient. Just writing about it makes me squirrely.

Karen Black also had strange looking eyes. I believe, as an actor, she was quite aware of her facial features. Her eyes are almost cross-eyed, her nose is super pointy, and her mouth is a bit askew. All these features make her intriguing to watch as she morphs into characters that scare the hell out of you.

The third story in the trilogy is actually an adaptation and screenplay written by celebrated horror writer Richard Matheson. Richard Matheson is credited as a writer for the movie. He was also a well-known writer for the famous, mind-bending TV show *The Twilight Zone*, which I still love watching when I can find episodes on streaming platforms. Richard Matheson was an influential writer, screenwriter, and author in the genres of horror, fantasy, and science-fiction.

In the movie *Barbarella*, we also had dolls with sharp, pointy teeth, exacting their terror on their prey. We know our creative minds can be subliminally influenced by what we read, hear, or see. Did that happen in the case of the Zuni Warrior Fetish Doll that has terrified countless people since they watched *Trilogy of Terror*?

Here we have another doll, biting, gnashing, drawing the blood of its human victim. What's up with that? Why do our minds have no trouble suspending disbelief, totally believing dolls come alive, hunt you down, and possibly maniacally torment and kill you?

Maybe it's because deep in the dark closets of our collective folklore, there have frequently been stories and tales of people using dolls to cause harm. The movies I cite in this chapter do an exceptional job of tapping into those collective, folkloric fears. It doesn't take much to believe if a human being can instruct a doll to do harm, the doll could also simply do harm of their own accord.

In *The Trilogy of Terror*, the doll comes with a warning not to remove the gold chain that keeps it from hunting, killing, doing unspeakable

harm, and inflicting terror upon its victims. Of course, the chain comes off, and the doll comes alive and proceeds to do what it was created to do. This is the terrifying paradox of the movie. The Zuni Fetish Warrior Doll has been captured, "bound," to use a magical term, not to cause harm by the gold chain. It doesn't take much imagination to believe whoever had the doll before it came into Amelia's hands knew the price that would have to be paid if the chain which bound the doll was no longer intact. We want to believe the Zuni Fetish Doll isn't capable of such acts. But it is. Some things are created for malevolent purposes. But darkness can be in the eye of the beholder. What if the fictional Zuni Fetish Warrior Doll was actually a "protector," made by its creator, but through the twists and turns of time fell into the wrong hands?

We know dolls are created by human beings. Some are made at the beloved knee of their maker, some are mass-produced in factories, some are made by children looking to create a playmate, and some are made using folklore and cultural instruction for a specific purpose. All dolls are made for a purpose. None are created "just because." A doll is made to be held, loved, to give comfort, become a confidant, a dear friend, a family member. But some dolls may have sharp, pointy teeth and tiny weapons from which you should stay far, far, away.

1988: Chucky: Child's Play

Director: Tom Holland

Writers: Don Mancini, John Lafia, Tom Holland

Release Date: 1988

Main Cast: Catherine Hicks as Karen Barclay; Alex Vincent as Andy Barclay; Chris Sarandon as Mike Norris; Brad Dourif as voice of Chucky (Charles Lee Ray); Dinah Manoff as Maggie Peterson

Awards: 2014 Saturn Award Winner—Best DVD/Blu-ray Collection; 1990 Saturn Award Nominee—Best Horror Film; 1990 Saturn Award Winner—Best Actress, Catherine Hicks; 1990 Saturn Award Nominee—Best Performance by a Younger Actor, Alex Vincent; 1990 Saturn Award Nominee—Best Writing, Tom Holland, John Lafia, Don Mancini

I have never felt an affinity for the Chucky doll or the Chucky movies. Personally speaking I have never felt drawn to the Chucky doll. There has never been a connection between me, the movies, and the doll. However, being the thorough researcher I am, in compiling my data for this book, on Sunday, June 16, 2024, my hubby, myself, and my three special dolls sat down and watched *Child's Play*.

As we watched the movie, I learned Chucky is a maniacal doll who inflicts harm. And just as my intuition and perceptions had always told me without ever seeing the film, the movie played the way I had anticipated. The only thing I was surprised by was the inclusion of "Voodoo." (Spelled this way because there is nothing authentic about the ritual in the movie.) This "Voodoo" ritual is how Chucky comes to life.

Chucky was not loved. He doesn't fit my definition of a doll for the purposes of this book. Chucky comes to life from the incantation of a demented serial killer who casts his spirit into the doll after being gunned down in a toy store. Oh, how sad. Sad for the toys, not the serial killer. There are many dolls in the store, and they bear painful witness to the ritual. As the camera pans across the dolls, you can feel their angst at what is about to happen. They know no good is going to come from this act.

After Chucky comes to life, I couldn't stop wondering: why is the Chucky doll so big? He's almost bigger than Andy, the sweet little boy in the film who longs for a "Good Guys" doll. Instead, he gets Chucky for his birthday and the rest is horror cinema history.

I realize this movie was released in 1988. At the time of this writing that was thirty-six years ago! I can totally see and understand how this movie would definitely scare the pants off anyone who doesn't love dolls, or who is easily scared by them.

But what sucks is that it is a Black man, cast as the "Voodoo Priest," who teaches Charles Lee Ray, the serial killer, how to use Voodoo to put himself into the doll. I did find it comforting that the Priest tells the Chucky doll, speaking to the human being he once was, that he is an abomination against nature. But Chucky turns the tables and uses "Voodoo" to kill the Priest.

The way Chucky changes from being a doll to a poorly animated character did little to make me love him. In fact, my dolls whispered to me, "He is an imposter." They are right. It's very sad Chucky turns on the little boy who did love him until he realized he was a doll gone bad.

Since it took me thirty-six years to watch this film, I won't spoil it by revealing the ending. I am assuming there may be others like me who have never seen the film and might be inclined to do so after reading this chapter. I also realize Chucky is an icon in the pantheon of doll movies. He has many fans who adore him and his ways. He is a popular Halloween costume, and his story is one that continues to live on in film and on the small screen. *Child's Play* may not have been for me, but we know every doll ain't for everybody!

Dolls need love. They need homes and a family to care for them. The serial killer obviously had none of that, and the lack of nurturing turned the "Good Guys" doll into a bad doll with the support of the ritual performed by the serial killer at the time of his death. I suppose it is entertaining to play with the belief that humans, even humans who commit horrible acts, can have a chance at immortality.

Chucky's spirit was definitely of a dark nature. It's an easy jump to think the character Charles Lee Ray, who cast his spirit into the doll, was never much loved as a person.

I won't be returning to watch the Chucky movies. This isn't the doll theme, or type of films that affect me, or I find endearing in that special way dolls can be for us. I was glad when the movie was over. However, the film does have its place in cinematic history as movies about scary dolls, which is why I included it in this chapter.

In the end, my dolls didn't like the way the Chucky doll turned on Andy. Andy is a sweet kid, and you find yourself rooting for him to get rid of Chucky.

Even though I didn't enjoy *Child's Play*, I am glad I did take the time to watch the movie. Knowledge is a good thing. I do thank my hubby and my dolls for spending their Sunday afternoon with me, watching the film.

1994: Claudia's Dolls: Interview with the Vampire

Director: Neil Jordan

Writer: Anne Rice

Release Date: 1994

Main Cast: Tom Cruise as Lestat; Brad Pitt as Louis; Kirsten Dunst as Claudia; Christian Slater as Malloy

Awards: Twenty-four wins and thirty-four nominations, featuring: 1995 Oscar Nominee—Best Art Direction and Set Decoration, Dante Ferretti Francesca Lo Schiavo; 1995 Oscar Nominee—Best Music and Original Score, Elliot Goldenthal; 1995 Saturn Award Winner—Best Horror Film; 1995 Saturn Award Nominee—Best Actor, Tom Cruise; 1995 Saturn Award Nominee—Best Actor, Brad Pitt; 1995 Saturn Award Winner—Best Performance by a Younger Actor,

Kirsten Dunst; 1995 Saturn Award Nominee—Best Director, Neil Jordan; 1995 Saturn Award Nominee—Best Music, Elliot Goldenthal; 1995 Saturn Award Winner—Best Costumes, Sandy Powell; 1995 Saturn Award Nominee—Best Make-Up, Stan Winston and Michèle Burke

Let's get personal. Sit back and relax while I take you on a journey into my past. We'll go back into a moment in time that forever changed my life and set my course on a trajectory from which I would never return.

In the late 1980s, I was employed as an administrative assistant in a hospital in Boulder, Colorado. I worked with a delightful group of powerful women who had the job of transcribing and taking meeting notes during important and critical meetings physicians and nurses held on a daily basis to discuss patient care.

My position taught me a lot about how insurance works. For instance, do you know as soon as you are admitted to a hospital, there is an entire work force that tracks how long you've stayed or are staying and how much, if any, your insurance will cover the cost of your admission. I also worked with the Risk Management team of the hospital in accordance with the Patient Advocates, who solely exist to help patients and their families when things go wrong during a hospital stay. All good information and knowledge that has helped me tremendously in my later years as an older person, a mother, and wife. I know a lot about insurance, hospitals, and how to get things done or who to contact when things go wrong, or not to my satisfaction for the care of my loved ones. Knowledge for which I am forever grateful.

As your life goes on, your memory and experiences fade to gossamer images and nostalgic emotions. It is highly possible you may not recall the names of co-workers with whom you had close relationships and who influenced you, but you can recall their faces. I do so now as I type these words. I can't remember her name, but I see her face, and I do recall she had beautiful long, dark, curly hair.

She was into the "vampire novels." She would bring a new book into the office and read it during her breaks. She was thoroughly engrossed and affected by them. She would share her feelings and emotions with me about the stories, but they just didn't do anything for me . . . at the time.

I wasn't into vampires. I liked witches, ghosts, and spirits, but the vampire world did not call my name. Their preternatural whispers blew right past my ears. But when they did call me . . . I answered and fell hard.

Fast forward to the early 1990s. I am employed in a part-time position as a receptionist in a trendy Denver, Cherry Creek hair salon. Those relationships would change my life. The salon was located in the swanky part of town, and the owner established himself as a leader in the hair care industry. He became known for his colors, and he also put on fashion shows around the city. I actually worked the runway for one of his shows and it was a night I'll never forget.

As people who work in salons tend to do, several of us in the salon became very close. The salon was our haven, our community, our day party gig, and workplace. And our clientele were name-dropping people.

I loved working for the hair salon in Cherry Creek. I was only there for a short time, but I still have close friends from that time in my life.

One evening, as we were closing the salon and I was finishing my chores as the receptionist, the owner asked me if I would like to go with him and other co-workers to see a movie. Sure! Why not? My schedule was free that evening and it was a glorious summer night in Denver. Absolutely, I would love to go.

"What's the movie?" I asked.

Interview with the Vampire.

Hmmm. A vampire movie? Okay. I was game. I remembered my administrative job in the hospital and the woman who loved vampire novels. It was my opportunity to see what all the hoopla was, and why people were so obsessed with vampires and those books.

I sat in the theatre, eagerly awaiting the film to begin. I was a bit nervous, too. It was clear to me a lot of people in the theater were excited about this movie, as they were fans of the author.

The movie started.

I felt a strange tingly feeling of awe and recognition as I watched the character Louis step into a cemetery, give himself over to Lestat, and a stone angel opened her eyes.

My whole mind whirled and my being expanded across time and space. It was as if someone had peered into the deep recesses of my magical, occult thoughts and put them on the screen. They had portrayed the world the way I see it.

I was fixated with the character Lestat and his blue eyes. I will admit that prior to this film I was not a Tom Cruise fan. I didn't like or dislike him as an actor. He just didn't do much for me. But when he had blue contacts in his eyes, and came on screen as the Vampire Lestat, I, I, I . . .

But what also seared into my heart was Claudia, played by Kirsten Dunst. I was completely transfixed by her character, and the doll she carried around with her. I also developed a longing to go to New Orleans, where I had never traveled to at that point in time, and which bore a hole in my soul.

Claudia becomes a killer vampire extraordinaire. She becomes a master at luring victims with her child-like looks and lonely attachment to her doll while she sits alone on a park bench in Jackson Square.

As the movie progresses, it becomes clear to Claudia that Lestat always gifts her dolls on her birthday. In one particular scene, she becomes enraged after receiving another doll on her birthday.

The dolls look oddly familiar. They all seem to look like Claudia. And Claudia, who was turned when she was a child, suddenly realizes she can never change.

And that's what we love about our dolls. They don't change, outwardly. They grow inwardly and become more valuable, loved, and

special to us over time. Of course, their clothes may change or become tattered. Their hair may fall out. But we still love them. And much to our happiness, there are wonderful, talented, skilled people who can help restore our dolls once they become tattered to their original lovely selves.

I was never the same after movie night with my salon co-workers. I am probably one of the few people from that time who had never read any of Anne Rice's books. After watching that film, I became obsessed with her Vampire Chronicles, and she became my favorite author of all time. I even set myself up to date a man with a blue eyes, something I had never done or been attracted to, and that man later became my husband! I'm still smitten by his blue eyes.

I did travel to New Orleans many times later in life, after my movie night experience and meeting my husband. New Orleans truly felt like a spiritual home for me. My husband and I have many wonderful memories from our travels to New Orleans.

I did get to meet Anne Rice before she passed away, at a book signing in my hometown of Denver, Colorado. She signed my favorite book from the Vampire Chronicles, *The Tale of the Body Thief.* It is one of my most treasured books. Anne Rice created a world for me I could escape to live in, believe in, and find respite, taking solace in her worlds, I could enter through the gates in my imagination. Her words were truly a gift to the world. Years later, when I finally set foot in the Crescent City for the first time on a magical trip with my husband, I felt I already knew it and belonged there as one of its dwellers.

I've watched the original movie, *Interview with the Vampire*, so many times I've lost count. I have an original VHS copy of the movie, even though our VHS player has long gone the way of relics. I love holding the box and looking at the cover, especially now in this day and age, when everything is released to digital formats.

When I watch the movie, still unto this day, my heart goes out to Claudia, played by Kirsten Dunst. She steals the scene, captivating us in her longing, hugging her doll on the lonely park bench. Of course, we know it is a setup for her victim, but the way she hugs her doll in the moonlight is how I feel about my dolls. They comfort you in the dark. They matter. They are magically alive and they're important.

Annabelle

2013: The Conjuring

Director: James Wan

Writers: Chad Hayes, Carey W. Hayes

Release Date: 2013

Main Cast: Patrick Wilson as Ed Warren; Vera Farmiga as Lorraine Warren; Lili Taylor as Carolyn Perron; Ron Livingston as Roger Perron

Awards: Fifteen wins and twenty-two nominations, including: 2014 Saturn Award Winner—Best Horror Film; 2014 Critic's Choice Award Nominee—Best Sci-Fi/Horror Movie; 2013 Hollywood Movie Award Nominee—James Wan

2014: Annabelle

Director: John R. Leonetti

Writer: Gary Dauberman

Release Date: 2014

Main Cast: Ward Horton as John; Alfre Woodward as Evelyn; Tony Amendola as Father Perez; Annabelle Wallis as Mia

Awards: Three wins and seven nominations, including: 2015 Saturn Award—Best Horror Film; 2015 MTV Movie Award—Best Scared-As-S**t Performance, Annabelle Wallis

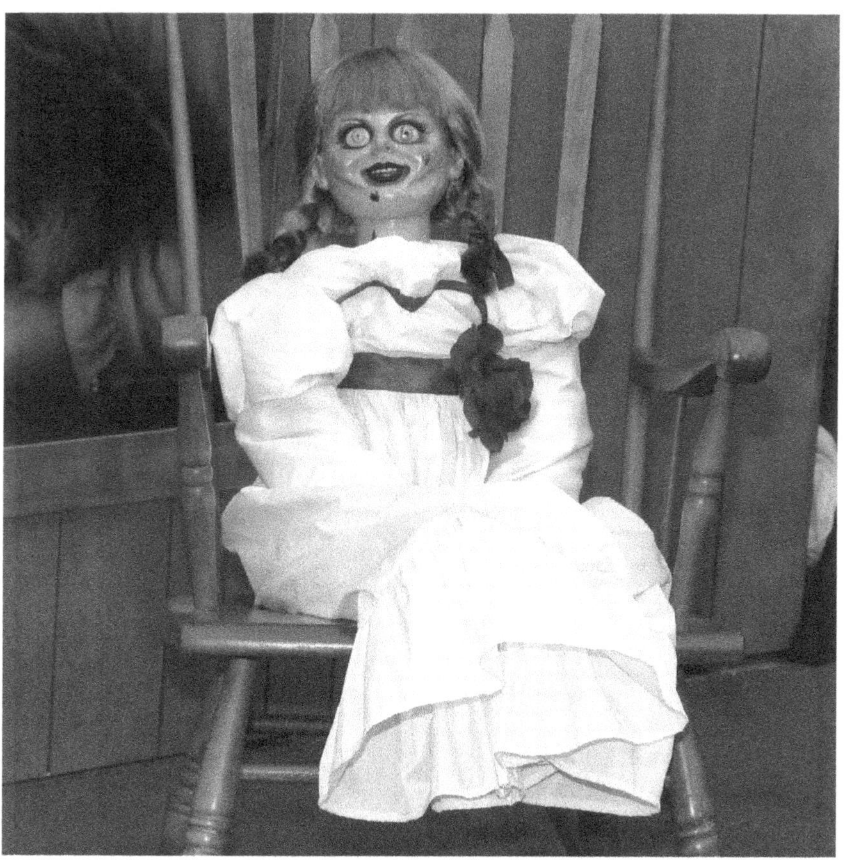

Prop Annabelle doll at Los Angeles premiere of 'Annabelle Comes Home' Regency Village Theatre, Westwood, California, on June 20, 2019.

Her very name stirs terror in the heart. Why are we completely fascinated and terrified by the doll named Annabelle?

Per my research, I discovered the Annabelle doll was originally made as a cloth doll. Later, the Annabelle name was given to dolls who mimicked children. We know dolls are made with human features, human hair, wigs, clothes that are made especially for them to be dressed as an adult, child, or infant. Some can also be made to walk, talk, or even dance! Understanding that dolls are created to represent humans in many different stages of life makes it possible for us to understand how dolls can seem to embody a human presence, or the spirits of children or adults.

Research shows the actual "haunted" Annabelle doll, as made infamous by the real-life investigations of Ed and Lorraine Warren, was a Raggedy-Ann doll. A video interview of the Lorraine Warren, a partner in the famous paranormal investigative team, and wife of Ed Warren, shows a display case housing the real Annabelle doll. However, the camera does not show the doll's face, which I found quite interesting and respectful. Personally speaking, I would not want to look into the face of the "real" Annabelle doll unless I had all my protective mojos and magick geared up for the experience. Forewarned is appropriate. Respect these dolls, we must.

We know the ability to be affected by what we watch or see in movies or on the small screen is great, especially if you are a highly intuitive, sensitive, and empathic person. I'm selective about what I watch. I know that what is scary or weird to me may be less scary or weird to others, or vice versa. We all bring our own point of view and personal experiences, to what we see, watch, or read.

The created, imagined Hollywood version of the Annabelle doll is a different story. Hollywood did quite the number on us, making movies where Annabelle the doll is a featured character. However, the Hollywood versions differ greatly both from the descriptions of an original

Annabelle doll, according to the entries in *The Collector's Encyclopedia of Dolls*, and from the real-life haunted Annabelle doll.

I can easily imagine a "mama" Annabelle doll creeping down a hallway, talking, walking or even dancing in a maniacal, threatening, terrorizing manner. *The Conjuring* and *Annabelle* both show Annabelle the doll magically moving from one place to another, and her screen presence is indeed haunting and threatening. She does have a way of getting under our skin. I do love the first *The Conjuring* movie. It is one of my favorite films!

But we also love Annabelle's ability to be enchanting and terrifying. If you are so inclined to love dolls the way many of us do, the on screen Annabelle doll does have a presence. In *Annabelle*, which gives us her backstory, Annabelle the doll comes to life from a drop of blood that spills into her eye during a horrific murder. There is also a disturbing connection made to the murder of Sharon Tate in *Annabelle*. I suppose this is what gives the film its hook into reality and a disturbing unsettling feeling, beyond the creepiness of Annabelle, the doll. I actually lived in Los Angeles during the time Sharon Tate was murdered. I was just a kid. It was and remains an absolutely horrid time in our history.

I wasn't convinced by the ending of the first *Annabelle* film, released in 2014. It was my second time watching the movie as part of research for this book. I had seen it previously on my own years prior, and I felt the same about it watching it for a second time. Alfre Woodward, who plays the role of Evelyn in the film, is one of my all-time favorite actors. I was not happy with her trajectory in the film. I mean, come on, now!

In *The Conjuring*, Annabelle the doll simply is haunted, casting her scary vibe offscreen, although she does make an appearance to let you know she is integral to the plot of the story. We see her put away for safe keeping by Ed and Lorraine Warren, in their personal museum where

they store all the possessions they've removed from their demonic and paranormal investigations. Even though the movie Annabelle doll looks nothing like the real Annabelle, she is still disturbing and unsettling to look upon. Good job, make-up and costume team!

Is it possible to love a doll enough for it to become alive? I think so, in terms of being alive in spirit, giving you a deep feeling of love and connection when you hold it, or look at it. Can a drop of blood from a demented, murderous individual bring a doll to life? Maybe. Perhaps. Or maybe only in the movies.

Personally speaking, from what I know about dolls, I doubt it. One would really need to be versed in the art of Conjure, using skills reminiscent of bygone ancient civilizations and hermetic societies. I believe one of my favorite lines from one of my all-time favorite TV shows, *The X-Files*, to be true: "Did you really think you could call up the Devil and ask him to behave?" That truly is the stuff of Hollywood movies, but it does make a good movie, and one that stays in your mind long after the credits have rolled.

Barbie and Black Barbie: The Motion Picture and the Documentary

2023: Barbie

Director: Greta Gerwig

Writers: Greta Gerwig, Noah Baumbach

Release Date: 2023

Main Cast: Margot Robbie as Barbie; Ryan Gosling as Ken; Issa Rae as Barbie; Kate McKinnon as Weird Barbie

Awards: One hundred ninety-seven wins and four hundred twenty-four nominations, including: 2024 Oscar Winner—Best Achievement in Music Written for Motion Pictures (Original Song); 2024 Saturn Award Winner—Best Actress in a Film, Margot Robbie; 2024 Saturn Award Nominee—Best Fantasy Film

2023: Black Barbie: A Documentary

Director: Lagueria Davis

Writer: Lagueria Davis

Release Date: 2023

Main Cast: Beulah Mae Mitchell; Kitty Black Perkins; Stacey McBride-Irby; Lagueria Davis

Awards: Two wins and four nominations, including: 2023 Best Black Lens Film Winner; 2023 Best Black Lens Film Audience Choice Award, Lagueria Davis; 2023 Greg Gund Memorial Standing Up Award Nominee

The original Barbie doll was created by Ruth Handler, an American businesswoman, in 1959. Interesting fact: Ruth Handler was born in Denver, Colorado, my home city, although as a child I grew up in southern California. My family moved to Denver in 1977, when I was a senior in high school, to the city of Colorado Springs. I attended Doherty High School in Colorado Springs, did a turn at the University of Colorado, lived in Boulder from 1977 to 1985, then I moved to Denver in 1985 to attend technical college, where I completed my degree in computer information systems. I am magical and technical. I've lived in Denver continuously since 1985.

As a child growing up in Southern California, in the enchanting city of Los Angeles during the 1970s, I listened to music that used words such as "magic," "spells," and "cast" to create positive, soulful vibes. Many of my childhood friends had Barbies, but a connection and fascination with them always seem to elude me. It actually made me kind of sad I didn't relate to Barbie dolls, as that excluded me from lots of fun play times with my friends, and their Barbies. For some reason, my imagination just couldn't make the leap into their world.

(I would also like to add as a child, I had a huge stuffed animal collection. I loved stuffed animals!)

When and if I did play with Barbie dolls, I would undress them and sit them naked in a window. Why? I have no idea. To quote the character Lydia from the 1988 movie *Beetlejuice*, "I myself am strange and unusual."

However, on a walk around Boulder several years ago, I saw a group of naked Barbies sitting in a window. It made my heart smile.

Maybe I didn't relate to Barbies because of their stick-like bodies and outfits. I wasn't a kid who was fond of dressing up dolls, which is mostly what my friends loved doing with their Barbie dolls. And Barbie dolls certainly didn't look like me. Remember my childhood began in the year 1960. The first Black Barbie doll wouldn't show up in the market until years later, when she was created by Kitty Black Perkins.

Fast forward to 2023, and the *Barbie* movie takes the world by storm. I will be honest; I had no intention or desire to see the *Barbie* movie. But being the thorough researcher I am, and of course recognizing the importance and significance of Barbie dolls, I coughed up the $23.00 (the most I've ever paid to watch a movie) and watched the movie on a streaming platform.

It was not one of my favorite films. Granted, I came to the film biased. Like I have shared, I did not play with Barbies as a kid. As an adult, one of my dear friends, who knows I love dolls, gifted me with a Black Barbie doll, Christie. She's still in the box. Maybe she is worth something!

I understood the plotlines and the story of the *Barbie* movie, and I get why the movie had global impact, but personally it did nothing for me. I didn't want to rush out and buy a Barbie doll. I'm sure that many did buy Barbies after watching the movie, though. And that is okay! Not every doll is for everybody. We all have our favorites. Just because Barbie isn't for me doesn't mean she isn't for you.

And then the fates of the Universe sent me a gift as I was writing this book. The giant streaming platform Netflix released the documentary *Black Barbie*. There on the small screen were all the things I had felt as a child and an adult about why representation matters in the doll world, along with the true story of the incredible undertaking to create a Black Barbie. I was fascinated with the story, and I applaud director Lagueria Davis for bringing the creation story of Black Barbie to the screen.

Although I deeply appreciated watching and learning Black Barbie's history, I still didn't feel called to purchase the doll. I simply don't have a connection to Barbies, Black or otherwise.

Perhaps it is because I don't feel the otherworldly presence I do in dolls that are created in the likeness and image of children. Most Barbie dolls are created to look like grown-ups or teenagers, with the exception of ones created to be her little sisters. They do not fit in my categories of why I am drawn to dolls. My dolls need a family. They need to be held and comforted. They are huggable. They have soulful eyes. They speak to me, whisper to me and I listen. I've never felt those connections with a Barbie doll. Barbie is an adult, ready to make her mark in the world. My dolls aren't ready for the adult world. They live in the childlike awe and fantasy realms of magic.

Notable Television Episodes Featuring Dolls

"Living Doll": The Twilight Zone, *Season 5, Episode 6*

Director: Richard C. Sarafian

Writers: Charles Beaumont, Jerry Sohl (uncredited)

Air Date: November 1, 1963

Main Cast: Telly Savalas as Erich Streator; Mary LaRoche as Annabelle Streator; Tracy Stratford as Christie Streator; June Foray (uncredited) as voice of Talky Tina

Talky Tina is not a fan of the little girl's stepfather in this episode of the classic science fiction show, *The Twilight Zone*. If you've never seen this episode of the original *Twilight Zone*, I suggest watching it. I also loved it because it is filmed in black and white.

It remains profoundly interesting to me how the imaginary worlds of television, theatre, and the arts can have a lasting impact on our psyches and collective pop culture consciousness.

The ability to suspend disbelief is a powerful tool. Logically we *know* what we're watching isn't real, but in that moment, it is truly real to us. We also know that when stories are grounded in real life, they are poignant, apt to have lasting effects upon us. It is easy to believe that in a small town, resplendent with pretty homes and white picket fences, there lived a little girl with a horrible stepfather, and to her rescue came a magical doll, a protector called "Talky Tina." We actually find ourselves rooting for the little girl and "Talky Tina."

"The Doll": Seinfeld, *Season 7, Episode 16*

Director: Andy Ackerman

Writers: Larry David, Jerry Seinfeld, Tom Gammill

Air Date: February 22, 1996

Main Cast: Jerry Seinfeld as Jerry; Julia Louis-Dreyfus as Elaine Benes; Jason Alexander as George Costanza; Michael Richards as Cosmo Kramer; Jerry Stiller as Frank Costanza; Estelle Harris as Estelle Costanza; Heidi Swedberg as Susan Ross; Kathy Griffin as Sally Weaver

In this hilarious episode of *Seinfeld*, which I still watch when I need all-out belly laughs, George, played by Jason Alexander, comes home to his apartment to find his fiancé, Susan, played by Heidi Swedberg, unpacking her furniture. She is moving in, and she is unpacking her doll collection. George is visibly disturbed, freaked out when he notices one of the dolls looks exactly like his mother.

(As an aside, in my personal doll collection, I do have several dolls people have gifted me over the years, saying the doll reminded them of me. I am always touched by their sentiment. A few years ago, I took a doll class where we learned how to make dolls from fabric. I had a lot of fun in that class, using materials like stones, curly strands of yarn, and buttons for eyes to make a doll I felt embodied the energy of the time and place of the class. It was fun crafting a doll with my own hands. I enjoyed being the maker of a doll to commemorate my experience. But none of my dolls actually *look* like me. That would indeed be a freaky situation!)

Susan doesn't see the resemblance in her doll, much to George's chagrin, so much so that one night she even brings the doll to bed with them, which completely disrupts their bedtime as a couple. Apparently, Susan is used to sleeping with her dolls. George, not so much, and definitely not with a doll who looks like his mother!

In the opening scene of this episode, Jerry, played by Jerry Seinfeld, has an annoying interaction with Sally Weaver, played by Kathy Griffin. Sally Weaver is actually Susan's old college roommate, and she has come to see Jerry's act which he is performing in her hometown, Memphis, Tennessee.

I always find it interesting, like finding hidden treasure, when you notice things in a TV show or film that aren't seen immediately. On the wall of the fictional club in Memphis where Jerry is performing is a poster with titles for an upcoming event. The words "Girls Bones Found" and "Little Monster" can clearly be seen. Fitting for an episode about look-alike dolls!

As the episode unfolds, George tries to get his friends to acknowledge the doll looks like his mother. In a hallway scene, Elaine, played by Julia Louis-Dreyfus, screams when she sees the doll. Further into the show, George declares the doll is spooky and freaking him out. Later the writers show us all dolls are not the same, when Sally Weaver brings Jerry a different doll than the one he requested (the doll who looks like George's mother) for his appearance on a TV show. He was going to use the look-a-like doll in a joke about George and his mother.

Finally in the last few scenes of the episode, George's father, Frank, played by the incomparable Jerry Stiller, loses control when he meets the look-a-like doll, who looks like his wife Estelle in person.

Off camera, we hear George's mother, Estelle's, voice speaking to Frank. Estelle's voice clearly triggers Frank and in a fit of hysterical rage, Frank rips the head off the doll! George ends the scene by reiterating to Susan in an "I told you so," moment, stating the doll did indeed look like his mother.

What a fabulous treatment of how dolls can impersonate and stand-in for living human beings, so much so that people triggered by their existence would rip their heads off! Another testament to the strange and wonderful life of dolls, and how they can affect us, as well as a warning if you have dolls who look like you, it may be best to keep them hidden.

"The Doll": Curb Your Enthusiasm, *Season 2, Episode 7*

Director: Robert B. Weide

Writer: Larry David

Air Date: November 1, 2001

Main Cast: Larry David as himself; Jeff Garlin as Jeff Greene; Julia Louis-Dreyfus as herself; Susie Essman as Susie Greene; Cheryl Hines as Cheryl David; Rita Wilson as Ann Michaelson; Bailey Thompson as Tara Michaelson; Ashly Holloway as Sammi Greene

Larry David is one of the co-writers and co-creators for *Seinfeld,* the infamously hysterical TV sitcom that aired in the 1990s. Larry David subsequently went on to create and star in his own show, titled *Curb Your Enthusiasm*, in which he plays himself.

In Season 2, Episode 7, we find Larry David attending an event where several network executives are also present. (In the opening scene we see Larry David sitting on a couch with Julia Louis-Dreyfus. I found it amusing that she makes an appearance in this show also titled "The Doll.")

In this episode, Larry David needs to use the bathroom. He finds himself in a predicament, because the door of the bathroom designated for guests is missing the lock. He tries in vain to figure out a way to use the bathroom and keep the door closed, but realizes he can't keep the door closed and use the toilet. The distance between the toilet and the door is too great.

In his search for a bathroom, he finds himself upstairs, asking if he can use the bathroom in the bedroom of Ann Michaelson's daughter, Tara, played by Bailey Thompson.

Tara is sitting on the floor, combing the long hair of her doll, named Judy. Her bedroom is filled with dolls. She and Larry David have a conversation about her doll Judy's hair, which ends with Larry David giving

her doll Judy a haircut. We notice Judy now closely resembles Tara who also has short hair.

At first Tara loves the haircut on her doll, but it doesn't take long for her to freak out and to run down the stairs screaming after she realizes her doll's hair will never grow back. Although there is no dialogue to suggest something else that may be afoot to cause such a reaction, as the audience, we do find ourselves wondering: does Tara secretly hate her own short hair? Maybe she wishes her own hair had never been cut.

Oh, the horror of a bad haircut! Children easily enter into the world where their dolls are living beings. It doesn't take much for us to understand why Tara would assume her doll's hair would grow back. After all, her hair grows after being cut. Why shouldn't her doll's hair grow back after a haircut? This reminds me of dolls from childhood, where you could pull longer hair out of the top of the doll's head. I still think of those dolls when I put my very long locs on top of my head in a ponytail. I love pulling the long pieces through the middle of the ponytail. It is truly amazing how the influence of dolls can follow us into adulthood.

In this scene with Tara and Judy, we see the magical relationship children have with dolls. Their dolls represent true friends, beloved family members. They are to be treated and cared for just like our "living" loved ones and friends. We further come to learn as the episode progresses that not only is Judy precious to Tara, she is also a collectible doll. Her value is priceless. She cannot be replaced.

To repair the damage which has been done, Larry and his best friend Jeff go on a mission to replace the short-haired doll. Jeff, who is separated from his wife, goes to his wife's home for a replacement doll from his daughter Sammi's collection. Jeff is pretty sure he has seen a doll that looks just like Judy with the short hair in his daughter's bedroom. After all, one Judy doll is like the other, or so they assume.

However, instead of taking the entire doll, they simply take the head! Another doll with her head ripped off. It does make me wonder, since

Larry David was also a co-writer on *Seinfeld*'s episode "The Doll," if he has a thing against dolls, since we are now watching a second story where a doll loses her head!

Susie Greene, Jeff's ex-wife, is furious when she realizes the head to her daughter's doll is missing. Their daughter screams when she finds her Judy doll doesn't have a head. Susie Greene accuses Larry and Jeff of doing some type of "voodoo shit," and demands Jeff and Larry bring back the original doll head.

Apparently, this family doesn't appreciate headless dolls in the same manner as the Addams family. (See page 86.)

In the end, Tara is happy with the new long-haired head on her Judy doll. However, during the transport of the head of the long-haired doll back to the home of Ann Michaelson, Larry stuffs the doll's head in his pants. He soon discovers he has incurred a rash on his private parts. Dare we say the doll didn't like being transported in that fashion, even if it was only her head?

Lesson learned, don't swap the heads on your dolls. One head cannot replace the other.

CHAPTER FIVE

History of Dolls in Magick

Poppets, Target Dolls, "Voodoo" Dolls

In the previous chapter, we focused on dolls featured in Hollywood movies and shows who have cemented their place in our minds and popular culture, and on their wide and great influence on us. This chapter focuses on the historical and magickal uses of dolls who fall into the categories of poppets, "target dolls," and "Voodoo" dolls.

The doll by its very nature lends itself to practices rooted in cultures and folklore as stand-ins or objects to be used to facilitate the desires of the magician or practitioner. A doll can be made to look like anyone or anything. Dolls can be made from fabric, clay, wax, mud, porcelain, or plastic. The materials used to create a doll are only limited by your imagination.

You have most likely come to understand by now, after reading several chapters in my book, I love movies. Let's look at another example of creating a doll by looking at another famous film!

One of the best portrayals in a movie, in my opinion, of a doll being created to cause harm as well as being a protector is from the movie *The Witches of Eastwick.*

When the three witches realize that their benefactor is *not* a good person—nor even an actual human person for that matter—they create a wax doll to banish him. The movie does an excellent job of teaching us what we need to use, to make a wax doll intended as a target, to banish someone we feel has become a harmful person or entity in our lives. Sometimes one must set a trap to catch an intruder.

Their wax doll does its job. Their benefactor is banished, but is he really gone? Was their magick successful or will they need to keep creating more dolls, and work to keep their protective boundaries intact?

As the movie comes to a close, as the audience we may never know the long-term final outcome between the witches, their benefactor and the children he sired, but we hope for the best.

In the movie *The Witches of the Eastwick*, the three witches are successful in creating a target wax doll.

Poppets

Returning to my love of movies, I must cite one of my favorite film series, *The Pirates of the Caribbean*, starring Johnny Depp, Orlando Bloom, Kiera Knightly, and Naomi Harris, who did a fantastic job playing one of my all-time favorite characters, the mysterious and beautiful witch Tia Dalma.

I would lovingly give myself over to be an apprentice to Tia Dalma. As soon as she emerges on screen, with her gorgeous hair—her locks filled with stones and powerful beads that hang down her back—and with her stunning sepia corset and gown, a heartfelt connection was made between her character and me. Kudos to the writers for their creation of this character and her home. She is one of the best parts of the film. However, though I have magically longed to apprentice under Tia Dalma, my heart tells me the cost might be a bit too high. Best not to write a spiritual check your soul can't cash!

A bit of a backstory about my love and affection for the *Pirates of the Caribbean* movies.

Growing up as I did the during the 1960s and 1970s in southern California, the California vibe gave me the sense magic was palpable and real. The radio played hit songs, which all seemed to convey something magical was going on in the ethers, and I breathed it all in. Everything seemed magical and possible. Not only did songs on the radio shape my childhood, but television was also dominant in creating magical worlds. The television shows *Dark Shadows* and *Bewitched* had tremendous effects on my desire to see and believe in magic. It's also fair to say I came into the world with these predilections. I consider it a gift from the Universe that my childhood coincided with genres of music and television shows that highlighted magic, mystery, love, and witchcraft.

Not too far from our home in Los Angeles was the city of Anaheim. Some of my fondest childhood memories are the summer family trips to Disneyland, and riding one of my favorite rides, The Pirates of the Caribbean. Disneyland is indeed one of my happy places. If I had stayed living in California, I have no doubt I would have eventually worked at Disneyland. I can see myself taking almost any job, just to become an employee at Disneyland.

As my memory serves me, the line to enter the ride was a long and windy queue, which seemed to go on forever. However, when you finally made you way inside the attraction, the atmosphere cooled instantly, and a faint mist seemed to blow in the air. It was fabulous. I recall boarding a boat that took us through ups and downs, twisting and riding through dark spaces. One of my favorite parts were the canons firing from the ships and the little dog that held the keys. A bow to Disney for giving those of us who actually rode the ride little gifts in the film. It was as if we shared a secret with Disneyland. Those of us who actually rode the ride knew when we saw the little dog holding the keys and the war going on

between the ships in the films, that those moments actually happened in the real attraction! Well done!

In the first movie, *Pirates of the Caribbean: The Curse of the Black Pearl*, one of the crew who is trying capture Keira Knightley's character Elizabeth says, "Hello, poppet."

I've always loved that scene. Of course, Elizabeth does not find the term endearing and flees for her life. But the moment the crew member speaks those words, you get a foreboding feeling, and you know this little poppet is in for trouble.

"Poppet" is an English term of endearment, especially used when referring to a young person or child. However, as magical people, when we hear that term, our minds go to a different place, the one which seems to be implied in the movie. As the movie continues, we come to realize the crew are not alive during a scene when moonlight cast upon the arm of a crewmember, and it reveals the arm of the skeleton.

In magickal terms, a poppet is a doll created from scratch materials, filled with items that will help the doll manifest the intentions you have placed within it. You could make a poppet for protection, a poppet for love, or a poppet to attract wealth, money, and success. Your poppets are only limited by your imagination.

Most poppets are made from fabric, which can easily be cut into a human shape, filled and stitched together without too much effort, and set to working by the power, practices, and beliefs of its creator. If making a poppet from scratch is not in your skill set, in this day and age you can easily buy an unstuffed muslin baby doll body from a fabric or craft store, ready for you to fill and dress to your desires!

I actually have one of these unstuffed muslin baby doll bodies. I've had it for years. I've never opened the package or used it. I like having it, but I've never felt called to open the package and make the doll. My affinities lie with dolls already created with a body, hair, limbs, eyes, and clothes, ready for someone to look after them and

care for them. But hey, it's good to keep your cupboards full of things you may never use but may have a purpose in your magickal future. Crafty people, such as witches and magical practitioners, tend keep everything. We keep used bottles, feathers, crystals, candles that may have only burned halfway down, buttons from old clothes, broken bits of jewelry, and dusty mason jars filled with herbs we may never use but feel we just might need someday.

All of these materials could be used in making a poppet doll. Perhaps it's my witchy senses that keeps the unused muslin doll body. It could come in handy one day.

Target Dolls

In my personal book collection is a book titled the *Encyclopedia of Magic & Superstition,* first published in 1974 by Octopus Books Limited, London. I find the dust cover of this book salacious in its portrayal of a Black woman holding a chicken. However, when you turn the page, you will find a beautiful, striking, purple image of the Eye of Ra, etched on the hard cover. The difference between the dust cover and the hard cover gives weight to the old adage, "never judge a book by its cover."

This encyclopedia is vast in its coverage of cultures and uses of magic coupled with superstition that humans have used to protect themselves for millennia. As I read through the pages I came upon the words "causing harm" in connection with the use or action of crafting dolls.

"Causing harm." A phrase that sends shivers up or down one's spine. Basically, a person creates a doll with the specific intention of causing harm, sending ill intentions or malice, to the target which the doll represents. The person is the target, and the doll is the arrow.

One of the best movies to represent the use of a doll as a stand-in for the victim is *Indiana Jones and the Temple of Doom*, starring Harrison Ford, Kate Capshaw, and introducing to us for the first time Ke Huy Quan,

who would later win an Oscar for his role in the film *Everything Everywhere All at Once*.

During one vibrant scene in *Indiana Jones and the Temple of Doom*, where Indiana Jones is being forced by Mola Ram to harm Willie Scott, played by the fabulous Kate Capshaw, the Little Maharaja can be seen sticking a pin into a doll, which is wearing a top hat and Western clothes. Every time the pin goes into the doll, Indiana Jones winces. The doll is the medium for sending pain to its target, Indiana Jones.

In another scene, as Doctor Jones is fighting for his life against a gigantic Guard, the Little Maharaja continues to stick a pin into the doll, to stop Indiana Jones from defending himself. The pin goes in, Indiana Jones winces in agony, and the Guard gains the upper hand in the fight. The cycle continues until Short Round, played by Ke Huy Quan, successfully stops the pin-sticking by delivering several blows and kicks to the Little Maharaja. You can't help but root for Short Round to beat up the Little Maharaja to make him stop sticking the dagger into the Indiana Jones doll.

Of course, we are given a good explanation. The Little Maharaja was also under an evil spell from Mola Ram, so his actions were not his own. He too was being controlled by an outside force. Using a target doll has consequences for its creator and the intended target.

"A hint to the wise is sufficient" is an old adage that carries great weight when one begins to dabble in things they don't understand or entertains ideas that they have the power to cause harm to others through the course of their own will by using a doll as a stand-in, as an image used to represent the person they mark as their target, or to be a representative of themselves.

This is not an over-simplification or a platitude, implying the world is nice place full of warm, loving, cozy people who only want the best for you, your family, friends, and loved ones. We know just by scrolling through social media platforms or listening to the news that the world is

and can be a scary, dangerous, and damaging place. Maybe you're not the type of person who would take the time and effort to create a doll with the specific purpose of causing or doing harm. I can't say that when we feel powerless or want to protect our family or loved ones from harm, or those seeking to cause them harm, that all sorts of magickal ideas may run through our heads. Perhaps this is why dolls have bad reputations for causing harm. They look like us and it doesn't take much to imagine why they could be used as stand-ins to inflict harm upon one's enemy.

History lays it down clearly and succinctly that since the beginning of our existence human beings can and have done horrible, at times even heinous, things to fellow human beings. It's not hard to empathize with why many people may want to have some control over the powerlessness, damage, or hurt they feel has been inflicted upon them. As noted earlier, dolls can be made from a myriad of materials, which may lend to their accessibility being crafted to use as targets, which seemingly makes them a readily available resource to address this powerlessness.

We find another great example of someone using a clay doll to inflict harm, power, and control in the movie *Stardust*, released in 2007 and starring Michelle Pfeiffer and Claire Danes. At the very end of the film (which I also love for its inclusion of a diverse cast in the villages and markets), Michelle Pfeiffer's character, Lamia, seeks to control Septimus, the last remaining brother of the family who seek to remain in power over the magical realm on the other side of the wall, which separates the mundane folk from the magical folk.

Septimus has already died. However, in Lamia's quest for eternal beauty, she is driven to extremes and picks up a clay doll and begins manipulating the limbs, which in turn manipulates and controls the body of Septimus to fight Trystan, the rightful heir to the throne. What is uncanny is that Septimus, along with his dead brothers, are watching this entire scene unfold from the realm of the dead, and he is clueless as to how Lamia is controlling his dead body.

Of course, these are Hollywood theatrics at its best. It is eerie and amusing to watch Lamia move an arm or a leg, and then see the body of Septimus repeat the same movements. However, in the end, the dead body of Septimus is destroyed, and Lamia pays the ultimate price for her insatiable greed. No good came to either party, with Lamia seeking to stay eternally young and beautiful, and Septimus trying to unrightfully claim the throne.

I do enjoy the story and the gorgeous cinematography, and it does almost make you believe you can create a doll out of clay and use it as a target to exact your will upon others. But ultimately, we know we are watching a fantasy film.

These films also tell us that the quest for power and greed, fortune, fame, and glory, and control over others can come at a costly price. The pirates in *The Pirates of the Caribbean: Curse of the Black Pearl* pay the high price in their quest for gold that did not belong to them. In *Indiana Jones and the Temple of Doom*, the priest of darkness and his soldiers pay the ultimate price for their skewed vision of power which they seek to obtain by stealing a precious and sacred stone from the villagers. And in *Stardust*, the greedy brothers and the witches pay the price of death and complete annihilation for their quest to be all-powerful and immortal. (Although I still wish witches didn't get a bad rap in the movies. Can't we be the heroine for once!) All these movies include the use of dolls or poppets to work the will of their creator.

These movies try to tell us to be forewarned. They point to a powerful secret . . . when you do those kinds of works, you bind yourself to that energy. It stays with you. And most people are so focused in casting the spell, they pay little to no attention as to how to clean up their mess (a line famously spoken in the movie *Practical Magic*) or protect themselves in the process.

So, if you choose to make dolls for targeted work, you best be sure this is the road you wish to go down. I cannot teach you how to make a

targeted doll. Instead, hopefully through my words, I have highlighted the history of dolls in magick, and how people have used and do use dolls as vessels for harmful intentions.

As a highly spiritual, intuitive, magical person, I do perform spell work and rituals on both a daily and seasonal basis that honor the seasons, the equinoxes, the morning and night, and the full moon. I find great joy in my childlike wonder and awe of the Universe. I find perspective, joy, healing, and comfort from simple things in nature, such as the birds that come to my feeder, crows flying overhead, a strong wind, or the sound of chimes. Watching white clouds in a blue sky soothes and inspires my imagination.

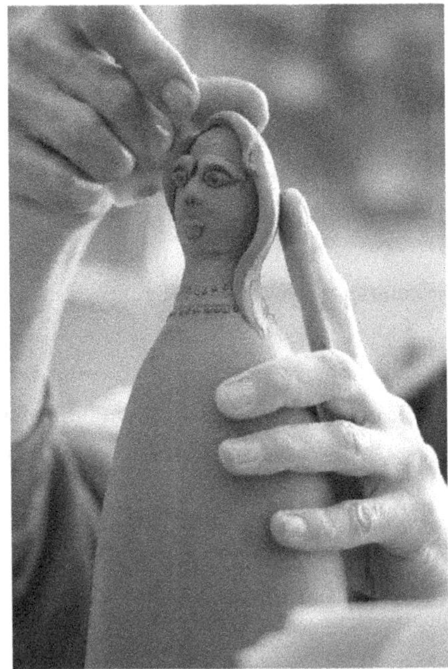

A wide variety of clay dolls can be created for target magic.

As a practicing witch, one who has been practicing my Craft for a very long time, I have learned through repetition, time, and practice what works for *me*. Every work or ritual I do, I do from the grounded center of my relationship with the Divine Mother Goddess, who for me is my Higher Power. I never enter into any magickal works without first entering into sacred space with my Higher Power, asking for guidance and protection. I take time to seriously contemplate what I may be deeming to undertake, why I am doing this magickal work, and whether it is in the best interest for me. Maybe it is. Maybe it isn't. Maybe I should sit with my thoughts for a while, contemplate my feelings, or take time to journal my emotions.

Anger is a true and valid human emotion. Anger can be fuel to help us move forward to create healthy boundaries or change situations which no longer contribute positively to our lives. A doll can become a trusted confidant for conversations when you feel angry, hurt, or resentful. However, taking that next step and turning them into arrows for targeted work is something one might give much thought and contemplation to before proceeding with such an act.

Most serious magical, spiritual people I know have a deep and abiding relationship with their Higher Power or Deities. As magical and spiritual people, we remain humble and in awe of Powers that are greater than ourselves. We take time to enter into ritual, prayer, or meditation to ask for guidance and protection before we set out on our paths to do magickal work. I would suggest the same efforts be given before you make dolls to use as targets.

"Voodoo" Dolls

I first set foot in the land of gumbo, muffalettas, and absinthe—also known as The Big Easy, the Crescent City, or simply New Orleans—in the late 1990s. My hubby took me down there for Mardi Gras, and it was a life-changing, life-altering experience.

We did all the things. We watched the parades, ate until we couldn't breathe, stumbled up and down Bourbon Street, and I "earned" a pair of golden beads that are priceless to me.

I fell in love with the city. By this time in my life, I had seen *Interview with the Vampire*, and was a passionate Anne Rice fan. On one fateful day while my husband was conducting business in the city, I went up to the Garden District neighborhood, where Anne Rice once lived, and took a cemetery tour. I'll never forget how I got turned around in the cemetery, and as I tried to orient myself at the end of a cemetery row, I saw a man wearing a top hat and purple sunglasses. The lenses in his glasses were round. I tried hard to find him again, but I never did. Was he a tour guide? Was he an apparition? I have no idea. All I know is I never saw him again. As I made my way out of the cemetery gates, he seemed to disappear just as suddenly as he had appeared. I truly felt as if I had stepped into the pages of an Anne Rice novel. The way he looked at me through his purple sunglasses, and then seemed to tip his top hat and disappear. Well, what can I say? It was my welcome to New Orleans.

New Orleans has a way of getting in your blood, especially for those of us who are drawn to the occult, history, magic, witches, vampires, folklore, good food, and the diasporic history of Black people. Over the next decade, my husband and I traveled to New Orleans for events, meetings, and business trips, so many times I lost count. In 2011, we had the blessed, magical experience of attending the very first Witches Ball in New Orleans, hosted by the marvelous Cairelle Crow Perilloux, author of *The Magic in Your Genes*. New Orleans is famous for its balls, many held

during Mardi Gras. It is also famous for the Vampire Ball, held in honor of Anne Rice and her beloved vampire fans, during Halloween season, but up until that time, there had never been a ball specifically for witches.

The 2011 Witches Ball was the stuff of dreams. It was held in the exquisite Van Benthuysen-Elms Mansion, located in the Garden District. Upon arrival, in the cool air of an October night, we were greeted by guests stepping down from horse-drawn carriages, dressed in their finest velvet, resplendent in gowns, capes, and top hats.

The dining room table was covered end to end with delicious, eye-dropping, mouthwatering New Orleans cuisine. Outside, on the garden patio complete with a stunning gazebo, was a full bar, where bartenders of the highest degree poured any libation your imagination could conjure.

There were tarot readers and a silent auction. I was thrilled when I won a black gazing mirror handcrafted by a New Orleans artist. The Witches Ball came to an end after the midnight ritual. In a heady state of enchantment, my husband, and our two dear friends, and I boarded the St. Charles streetcar and tripped the light fantastic in the French Quarter until dawn beckoned us that it was time to go home. Oh, such fond memories! New Orleans had cast its spell upon me.

I was so smitten with the city of New Orleans that when an opportunity arose for a promotion in my professional career as an IT Specialist working for the federal government, I applied for and was hired by an agency whose headquarters were in New Orleans. I was super blessed during my career to travel to New Orleans for business, and I also made lovely friendships with a group of extraordinary witches, who invited me to keep the full moon with them. At one point in my life, prior to my retirement from federal service, I tried very hard to extricate myself from my Mile High city and take up permanent residence in New Orleans, but the Goddess had other plans for me. I never did get to move to the Crescent City and live in a shotgun house. (So-called because these rectangular southern-style houses are arranged in a straight line with one room

leading right into another. In theory, at least, if the doors between rooms were open, a bullet fired from the front door could leave through the back without touching a wall.)

At times my affair with New Orleans feels bittersweet, tinged with the emotions of an unrequited love. *C'est la vie*!

From my journeys and trips to New Orleans, as well as through the influence of my studies with mystical teachers and spiritual leaders, I came to know the Divine Marie Laveau. I became fascinated, enchanted, and inspired by her life story. I am always searching for representation and the Divine Marie Laveau called out to me. During one business trip to New Orleans, I was able to find time to visit Marie Laveau's grave and leave an offering. I will always remember bowing before her tomb, helping to clean up offerings, and the blessing I received from her tomb's caretaker. I remain grateful I was able to have this solo, precious, magical, ancestral experience. This life-changing experience occurred before the tragic event of her tomb being painted pink. Thankfully the cemetery was able to restore her tomb, but the event forced the cemetery to only allow visitors to the Divine Marie Laveau's tomb in the presence of a tour guide, which is highly understandable and appropriate, given what had happened to her tomb.

The Divine Marie Laveau is very special to me. I think of her as a spiritual ancestor. In my book, *Powerful Juju: Goddesses, Music, and Magic for Comfort, Guidance, and Protection,* you will find an entire chapter devoted to working with her.

I keep a statue of the Divine Marie Laveau on my mantle. I have paintings of her in my living room.

Throughout all these journeys and experiences, which include many trips to New Orleans, and establishing a deep, spiritual connection with the Divine Marie Laveau, I have never felt the need to create a voodoo doll. Interesting but true fact.

It is common knowledge you can buy pre-made voodoo dolls anywhere and everywhere, online and in brick-and-mortar stores, or you can

make one for yourself, if you are so inclined. I may have strong feelings in this area because, personally speaking, the thought of a sticking a pin into one my dolls with the intention that those stabs be arrows of baneful magic creeps me out. I would never use them for that purpose.

During one of our trips to New Orleans, we also visited the Oak Alley Plantation. This was my first and only visit to a plantation. It took me most of my life to get up the nerve to go on a "plantation tour." I didn't know if I would be able to cope with the emotions I knew that I would experience visiting a plantation and its history of slavery. I knew there would be much my heart would have difficulty processing. I knew visiting a plantation would stir deep emotions within me. Yet, I am glad we took the tour. Once was enough.

After I fell in love with the movie *Interview with the Vampire* and Anne Rice's novels, I came to know that Oak Alley Plantation was used as a movie location in the film. The magnificent oak trees which grace the long driveway, leading to the Oak Alley Mansion, are famous.

We took the tour on a bright, clear, sunny day. I vividly recall that, as we drove down the two-lane road, I looked out the passenger side window, and two Black people, an African-American man and woman, were riding bicycles along the top of the levee. They waved at me.

I was so touched by that gesture! I felt as if my long-lost cousins were waving to me, and I was being welcomed back home.

The plantation tour was emotional. I had to hold back my tears many times as we toured the slave cabins and the interior of the mansion. I will always remember the tour guide explaining to us the job of an enslaved little boy was to pull the string on a giant bamboo fan back and forth to cool the slave owners as they ate at their grand table.

These collective memories and experiences stay with me. It may be why I've never felt drawn to create or use voodoo dolls. I only speak for myself and not the practices of others.

As a lover of paranormal, occult, films, and movies, one of my favorite movies is *The Skeleton Key*, starring Kate Hudson, Joy Bryant, Peter Sarsgaard, Gena Rowlands, and Maxine Barnett.

I love this movie. I love the eeriness, the sets, the names of the characters, Papa Justify and Mama Cecile, and the real Hoodoo products used in the film.

I also love how Jill, played by Joy Bryant, tells Caroline, played by Kate Hudson, as she prepares to enter a Hoodoo shop that Vodou is a religion, and Hoodoo is folk magic, but she isn't going to mess around with it. I also find it interesting that, in the scene, there are no voodoo dolls for sale in the shop, although there are plenty of candles and herbs for sale. You would think voodoo dolls would be clearly seen as an item for sale.

Later in the film, Caroline shows photos of dolls to Luke, played by Peter Sarsgaard. We can clearly see that as we look at the photos, through the lens of the camera, the dolls in the photos are not the kind you want to cuddle and hug.

Further along in the movie, we do see a voodoo doll show up in nightmare imagery. I won't spoil for it you if you haven't seen the movie.

We also take space on this page to give our condolences to the late Maxine Barnett, who passed away in December 2020. Maxine shone in her role as Mama Cynthia, the Hoodoo shopkeeper, in *The Skeleton Key*. Her performance nails the authenticity of the film for me. She is only on screen for a few minutes, but she nails her character. Her scene as the shopkeeper and the presence she conveys always makes me wish I could have met her movie character in New Orleans and spent some time in with her in her brick-and-mortar shop. I also love that they cast the Hoodoo shop as being in the back of a laundromat. It's hidden in plain sight. If you know, you know.

I also love the bones hanging in the doorway of the gas station in an earlier scene in the movie. I always think about doing the same on my front porch. I haven't done it yet, but it could happen!

I know the word "voodoo" conjures all types of pernicious visions of the haunted and scary. A lot of us like to be scared without deeply diving into the real thing. Sure, it's fun for a day or on Halloween to be scary, and pop some popcorn for a night at home watching movies while you get the shivers and chills, but most people will shy away from real and authentic practices.

This doesn't mean you can't buy voodoo dolls in New Orleans. Having fun is a good thing. In fact, laughter can do wonders to heal a sad day. Sometimes I like to watch creepy movies when I'm feeling down. And I love it when the weather changes to foggy, cold, and dreary. In Colorado, we don't get much in the way of fog, but a foggy day is a treat, and I do love cold and chilly weather.

One of my favorite books I read as a kid was about a little girl who visits and has friends that only appear in the fog. I loved that book! As the years passed and I became an adult, I found myself haunted by the story, but I could never remember the title. I could hardly believe it when social media came to my rescue! One day I posted about the book and almost immediately someone replied with the answer! The book is *Fog Magic,* by Julia L. Sauer.

For years, I thought the book didn't exist. I was so happy to find it actually is a real book. And to add to my magical foggy blessings, I found an original copy online! Of course I ordered a copy right away. As life would have it, when the book arrived, I was recovering from surgery. I held onto it until I was in the right frame of mind to read it. It was just like I remembered as a child. The magic was still there in the pages of the book. Reading the book as an adult reminded me of how powerful a story can be, or the power of a childhood doll you carry with you into adulthood. Stories, books, and dolls can exist for a long, long, time.

The only voodoo doll I have in my collection, I purchased in a tourist shop in New Orleans. I was walking down a street in the French Quarter,

window shopping. Window shopping is a fabulous way to spend time in New Orleans. Oh my gosh, there is so much to see!

My little doll was sitting, posing pretty in a window. I knew she was a novelty. I thought she was fun, but I never felt any magical or spiritual connection to her. She was a cute little doll, and I liked her clothes and button eyes, and I thought she would look cute on my work desk. She lived on my desk at work for a long time, in fact until I retired from federal service. Keeping her on my desk, in plain view of all my coworkers, was a source a fun for all of us. Of course, most of my colleagues at that time were from New Orleans, so they too enjoyed the sentiment.

On a serious note, people from all walks of life and magical practices do create voodoo dolls. A quick internet search will return a plethora of images of what a voodoo doll looks like, and how to make one. They all tend to look the same: a cloth figure, hand painted or handstitched with human attributes, and they usually have a pin or pins, so you can stick and work the doll with your intentions for your intended target. I feel safe to say many are created just for fun, but I'm sure some are created so they can be set to working on behalf of their creator.

Just because I've never made one doesn't mean belief in their powers isn't strong and long-lasting. Just because I've never made one does not negate the fact there are practices and practitioners who use voodoo dolls and consider them to be powerful, magical talismans.

However, most people tend to look at them as a novelty or as a tourist purchase they made on a trip to New Orleans. If you do wish to create a "real" voodoo doll to use for whatever intentions you may have in mind, I would suggest finding the proper spiritual person to assist you in your journey. I can't tell you how to do that. That journey will be up to you, and your desires, and maybe a trip to New Orleans. Not everything can be learned from reading a book. As with all things of a serious and magickal nature, respect and humility will carry you a long way.

CHAPTER SIX

Fascinating Doll Locations

During my research for this book, I came across people, places, and stories that grabbed my attention.

Some are well known places, a few are off the beaten track, and others came to me personally when my dolls and I appeared as guest speakers or presenters at conferences, such as the 2023 Occult Humanities Conference at NYU in New York, New York; the 2023 Mystic South Conference in Atlanta, Georgia; and the Between the Worlds: Sacred Spaces Conference in Baltimore, Maryland in 2023. I am truly grateful to the people who have shared their love of dolls and doll stories with me, and the places I have yet to visit but that call to me with me their folklore and magical histories. Here are some of the magical doll locations that exist.

Isla De Las Muñecas

The name *Isla De Las Muñecas* translates to "Island of the Dolls." This island is located in Xochimilco, Mexico, which is just outside Mexico City. After watching videos about Isla de las Muñecas, which pinpoint the location as being near Mexico City, the urge to see it with my own eyes is

even stronger. I too would like to experience a ride in the colorful boats drifting down the waterways leading to Isla de las Muñecas.

Many legends, fables, and stories about Isla de las Muñecas abound. Isla de las Muñecas has become a place of myth, urban fantasy, and legend. You will need to use your intuitive discernment to decide what is true, and what has been spun into creation by tourists and visitors to the Island. If you do get to go, hopefully you'll post a reel or create a video, so we can all see what you thought of your experience of the island. I also found it interesting that there now exist fake Islands of the Dolls. People will do anything to cash in on a story. But that also makes getting to the real island part of an exciting adventure.

The dolls of Isla de las Muñecas

It's generally agreed that, in the year 1950, a man by the name of Julian Santana Barrera came upon a small girl in the river. I'm not sure how she ended up in the river, but sadly she drowned. (Some stories say it was a little girl who drowned, other stories say it was an adult woman. I tend to believe it was a little girl who passed away, based on the baby dolls Mr. Barrera hung all over the island.) Later, Julian found a doll floating in the river, near the same location where the girl had passed away. To appease the spirits of the island, and to honor the little girl, he began hanging dolls from trees and branches and all over the wooden structure that was his home.

Julian Santana Barrera passed away at the age of eighty-six in 2001, and is buried on the island. Mr. Barrera collected dolls for more than fifty years, hanging them in the trees and in his hut to appease the ghosts which showed up after the little girl passed away. Other sources state that he hung up the dolls to honor the little girl who passed away.

As a doll lover myself, I choose to believe the legends and stories which say he was honoring the life of the little girl by displaying dolls hanging from the trees and posted on buildings on the island. We know dolls are comforting. Should you choose to watch videos of the island, you will see that once a doll was hung up, she was never taken down. This makes me think of a story of mine involving a pair of sunglasses. Don't test Spirit. If you travel to the island, it's important to be respectful to the dolls and leave them at their location. I couldn't imagine someone removing a doll from the island. It gives me the shudders just thinking about such an act.

I found it sad to see words such as "haunted," "creepy," "scary," or even the word "Voodoo" used to describe people's impressions of Isla de las Muñecas, though one might feel scared or haunted by the dolls if they're not your thing, or you don't understand their purpose for why they live on the island. Mr. Barrera's final resting place is on the Island. I'd definitely say Isla de las Muñecas is deserving of admiration and respect.

The dolls of Isla de las Muñecas

I found it comforting to see that visitors to the Island have left money and candles, as an homage to Mr. Barrera and the dolls. One video shows footage of an altar made for one of Mr. Barrera's favorite dolls. Scary? Creepy? I chose the word "sacred."

Muchas gracías to the fabulous travel bloggers who have recorded their trips to this uniquely awesome, mysterious, and wondrous place. You can find plenty of videos of this island online.

As world travelers, my husband and I have traveled to beautiful Mexico many times. The flights from Denver to the beach resorts of Mexico are relatively inexpensive and flight times aren't usually more than a couple of hours.

It's such a treat to wake up on a cold, snowy Denver morning, and have your feet in the *azul* waters and gorgeous sands of magnificent Mexico by noon. I love looking out the window as we fly over tropical trees and blue waters, preparing for landing. As the runway comes into view, our senses began to adjust, change, and align with the much needed warmth and respite of Mexico. We try to book flights leaving Denver early in the morning and the flight crews always do a great job of creating a festive atmosphere on the plane. By the time we land we've already thrown back a few cocktails and are ready to hit the streets and beaches of Mexico!

I also speak conversational level Spanish. Traveling to Mexico is an opportunity for me to get past my shyness and speak Spanish as we enjoy our vacation. I always feel a bit a shy at first to speak Spanish in Mexico, because I don't want to offend anyone by speaking incorrectly. However, I have found once I get started, the Mexican people are so very gracious, and soon I am communicating with ease. On many trips, once they learn I speak Spanish, they won't allow me to speak English. It is a real treat and a boost to my language skills.

(Here's a tip for world and international travelers; learn at least a few basic words such as "please," "thank you," "hello," and "goodbye," in the

native language of the country you are visiting. Even if you flub up or make mistakes, the people will appreciate the effort. Once they know you can say a few words in their language, you may find your trip takes on a more friendly vibe as you interact with locals, rather than just being a tourist.)

Our favorite places to visit thus far are Puerto Vallarta, located in Jalisco, and the island of Cozumel, located in the state of Quintana Roo. Puerto Vallarta combines the energy of an ancient city with the tranquility of chill beaches and calm waters. It maintains a sense of ancient history along with a welcoming vibe. On one trip, we passed a stunning woman who had eyebrows just like Frida Kahlo! On another trip we toured a weaving factory where highly skilled women still wove cloth on vintage, antique looms. It was mesmerizing to watch them create colorful scarves and fabrics.

An added treat we found while visiting the city of Puerto Vallarta is the seaside town of Mismaloya, which feels as if you've stepped through the portal of time into another world. To get to the beach in Mismaloya, one must walk down a tiny road, filled with local dive shops on one side of the road, and gorgeous flowers in stunning magnificent colors of pink, magenta and yellow climbing up stone walls, with luscious green trees on the other side, which create an ethereal tunnel as you make your way to seashore. Just writing about it now brings back such wonderful memories. We truly have a soft spot for Mexico and its beautiful cities and towns.

Once you reach the beaches of Mismaloya, you will find little tables adorned with thatch umbrellas gracing the shoreline, ready and waiting to shade you from the sun. It's super easy to find a table, order a delicious coco-loco, which is a heady brew made from different types of alcohol and fruit punch served in a coconut with a straw, and sit by the water and watch the waves roll in and out, all day. Drink enough of them and you too will be coco-loco. Ah, Cozumel!

The island of Cozumel is a world class diving destination. Although I am not a scuba diver (going into the deep waters of the ocean is not for me), I am a great snorkeler. I can snorkel for hours. I love staying close to shore, yet far enough into the water to see all the beautiful and amazing fish that live in the Gulf of Mexico. It's amazing what you can see just by putting your face in the water. And if you feel comfortable venturing out a bit further, the rewards are certainly worth it. On one snorkel trip, I ventured out into the water farther than I normally go and was rewarded with a view of a reclining stone goddess, sitting on the ocean floor.

Although I've been a mountain city dweller, having spent my entire adult life living in Colorado, I feel most at home near bodies of water. I've always thought that if only Colorado had an ocean, it would be perfect! Even though we are not a beach front property state, I do love seeing the rushing waters of our rivers and streams and our pristine mountain lakes. It's hard to put into words the awe and wonder I feel whenever I travel "up" to the mountains and sit by a Colorado river, stream, or lake.

The resorts located near beaches are my favorites in Mexico. However, on one occasion we traveled to remote Huatulco, in Oaxaca. Huatulco will always be memorable for its jungles, butterfly pavilions, and delicious fresh seafood. I'd also love to share a story about the time the ocean goddess of Mexico took my stunner shades from me. This story may shed some light on why I know first-hand you must be respectful when addressing entities and magical places. There is no better teacher than having your naivete knock you literally on your ass.

On a trip to Mexico, I decided to take a candle made in the shape of a goddess to leave as an offering to the ocean. During the trip the candle became damaged. It wasn't completely broken but one part of the wax was cracked. I tried gingerly to hold the candle together when I placed it on the sand and lit the wick. When I saw the flame burning, I was

confident my offerings had been received. I was happy I was able to leave an offering.

The next day we were hanging out on the beach, dipping in and out of the ocean waves. I was wearing my favorite shades, a pair of Vera Wang sunglasses that were deserving of their own place on an altar. They were the only true piece of designer fashion I had ever owned and were one of only four pairs of Vera Wang sunglasses that were sold in Denver when I purchased them.

I stepped into the water looking cute and sassy wearing my Vera Wang sunglasses. All of the sudden, out of nowhere, a rogue wave crashed upon me and threw me around like a rag doll in a washing machine. When I emerged from being tossed around in the water, my sunglasses were gone, and my bathing suit was full of enough sand to build a three-story sandcastle.

The goddess of the ocean had taken my sunglasses! To this day I imagine a mermaid swimming around in the ocean depths wearing my Vera Wang sunglasses, saying, "I look good in these!"

Lesson learned. Never offer a broken candle! I mourned my Vera Wang sunglasses for years.

I've yet to grace Mexico City, but it is definitely on my list of places to visit, especially during the celebration of Día de los Muertos. As old school Denver folks, we have our favorite restaurants for Mexican food. We go to one restaurant for green chile and chicharrónes, another for homemade tortillas, refried beans, and barbacoa, another for carne asada, and another for tortas! I would love to wander Mexico City while stopping in one restaurant after and another, filling up on Mexican cuisine as we tour the multitude of shops and dazzling colorful bars.

Our beautiful Denver Botanic Gardens always holds a mesmerizing display of Catrinas and Day of the Dead creations during October to celebrate the rich culture and history of Mexican people. This year, the Gardens held a magical exhibit titled Spirit Guides. Per

BotanicGardens.org, it's described as "a traveling exhibition featuring eight outdoor sculptures by the workshop of contemporary Mexican artists Jacobo and María Ángeles. Inspired by Zapotec astrology, these brightly colored and richly patterned sculptures depict fantastical hybrid animals that act as both spirit guides and astrological embodiments of human character."

I am a member of the Denver Botanic Gardens, which is one of my go-to places for spiritual nourishment and replenishment. The Spirit Guides exhibit was one of the best ones I've ever attended. I went twice. I now have my own unique one-of-a-kind Spirit Guide, which I purchased exiting the exhibit. I was excited to bring a little Spirit Guide home with me. It now graces my desk and inspires me to carry on with my magical writing!

If you've read my book *Powerful Juju,* you know I have a deep love and affection for Frida Kahlo. One of my dreams is to manifest a visit to her Blue House (*Casa Azul*) in Mexico City. I've watched the movie *Frida,* starring the stunning and talented Salma Hayek, so many times I've lost count. I own several works of art featuring Frida Kahlo, made by artists in her honor. One of my favorite pieces is an altar kit I purchased when I toured the Frida Kahlo exhibit at the Philadelphia Museum of Art in 2008. Perhaps a trip to the Island of Dolls and Frida Kahlo's Blue House during the time of Día de los Muertos is in my future!

On another note, as I watched videos about Día de los Muertos celebrations, particularly in and near the city of Patzcuaro, I was touched by footage of people, family members and beloveds of the dearly departed, dancing and drinking, holding parties and lively celebrations in the cemeteries, on around the graves of their loved ones who have passed away. Western culture seems to steer clear of anything that connects a sacred celebration to death. On October 31st, I like to say, "Happy Halloween. Blessed Samhain!" While Halloween is a multi-billion-dollar secular celebration of the haunted, chilling, and spooky, Samhain is a

sacred time of remembering our loved ones who passed on, crossed over to the other side.

I create my Samhain altar to honor the memory of family, friends, and loved ones who have died. I may choose to place their actual photographs on the altar, or I may use a blank frame to represent all of them. I may place seasonal flowers on the altar, candles in the shape of skulls, favorite foods or candies, or cherished mementos. I may light candles and say their names.

But in recent years several people very dear to me have passed over, and I have found myself not ready to create an elaborate altar in honor of their passing. My grief is still too fresh. And that's okay. I can still find joy in the silly, fun, celebration of Halloween. I also have a personal ritual where I pour a bit of water in honor of my loved ones every morning. They are always with me, and I always carry my love for them and their love for me, with me. If I don't feel called to create an actual Samhain altar on October 31st, I am totally fine with not doing it. In all things magical, secular, and religious, we must allow people to process their grief as it ebbs and flows for them, naturally.

I do appreciate the cultures of the world that celebrate death as part of life. I sincerely wish those cultures and celebrations continue to thrive, so we may learn from their examples, as we find our ways to celebrate and honor the death of our loved ones. Maybe Mr. Barrera was also leaving us clues about how to honor the Dead. His dolls are a testimony to the power a doll can bring into the lives of those seeking comfort. He must have been comforted by their presence as he kept acquiring them and he was laid to rest on the island. If he found dolls creepy or scary, I'm sure his final resting place would be located anywhere else, not on the grounds of his beloved Doll Island.

Ed and Lorraine Warren Museum

There is something special about Ed and Lorraine Warren, the famed medium couple who investigated cases such as the Amityville Horror. Though I never met them in real life, even the way their names sound together when you speak them aloud is magical. I feel it is safe to say that I, along with thousands of others, hold admiration and wonder for the fascinating and powerful influence Ed and Lorraine Warren left upon the world. If I could have had the pleasure to sit and talk with them, I would have jumped at the opportunity. I can only imagine our conversations and perhaps the knowledge they may have chosen to share with me. I sincerely hope they would have recognized me as a "true believer."

The Warren Museum, which was a collection of haunted items obtained by the Warrens over the course of their investigations, is housed in the basement of the home where Ed and Lorraine lived in Monroe, Connecticut. Unfortunately, the Warren Museum is permanently closed. The Museum closed permanently when Lorraine Warren passed away in April 2019.

A quick and easy internet search will return countless videos about the Warrens, some of the best being ones filmed by their son-in-law Tony Spera, along with a very touching interview with Lorraine Warren and Heather Halley from Gravity Media, titled *Lorraine Warren's Last Interview: Her Final Words of Wisdom.*

In this interview Lorraine shares her feelings about *The Conjuring,* the original film in the extended *Conjuring* universe, which you now know is one of my all-time favorite films. Lorraine states, "The movie was very well done, very well done, very, very, well done." Since I have such an affection for *The Conjuring,* it makes me happy to know Lorraine Warren approved of the film. I also found it interesting Director James Wan states in his interview, *The Conjuring: James Wan & Lorraine Warren Official Interview Part 1* from ScreenSlam: "It was less scary to build a set of the house." Even James Wan knew he was not a person who should step

into the shoes of Ed and Lorraine Warren, who were skilled and highly respected paranormal investigators with years of training, and healers of intense, terrifying negativity in the lives of real people.

James Wan made a great film based on the experiences of Ed and Lorraine Warren, but he is clear about his role. He is the filmmaker. James Wan excels in his field, as did the Warrens. Movies are one thing; real life is a completely different ball game. Personally speaking, I now have some experience being on set and being cast in a movie. A movie set is filled with lots of people; actors, technicians, a lighting crew, a sound crew. There are people moving back and forth constantly, except for when the director calls, "Quiet on the set!" The environment is well controlled. I would imagine being in a house under the influence of extreme negative energies would be quite disturbing and intimidating.

As I watched and re-watched several videos regarding the Warren Museum, Lorraine Warren made it clear the museum was actually *not* in the basement of her home. To gain access, one went through a passageway that connected her home to another building or outcropping where the museum was housed. The museum was located on her property, but not directly connected to her house.

During my research, it became clear that many videos and stories liked to make it appear the museum was in their home. That indeed would be scary. I believe that having *respect* for the occult and paranormal, or things we deem supernatural or otherworldly, can carry you a long way. I may not understand a lot of it, and I try to keep myself humble, as there are things in the Universe of which I have no idea of their power or influence. I have also learned to let go, as many things of a paranormal, haunted, or supernatural nature ain't for everybody, either. It is good to stay in your own lane.

As seekers, we may find ourselves in situations that, from the outside, we thought were going to be okay. These are situations when, looking at them from the perspective of an outsider, we thought

they would be in alignment with our spiritual values. It is completely acceptable if you find yourself in a situation, be it magical/magickal or mundane, which you thought was going to be a positive experience for you and it turns out to be otherwise, to give yourself permission to leave and never return. To thine own self be true is never more valid than in these types of situations.

It is generally accepted human beings come into contact with spiritual energy of all types. Spiritual energy taps into our emotions. We can recognize it as a *deja vu* feeling, or an intimate sensation which feels real and valid to our soul. No one can explain why we have these connections or "a-ha" moments. We simply do. One type of spiritual connection which comes to mind is the popularity of mediums who reach out to loved ones on the other side. Is that for real? Are these people true? I believe yes. Some people are truly gifted in making connections to the other side, allowing themselves to become portals for communication.

In the end, it is up to you to decide if the information being passed to you rings a bell. I've had a few readings with gifted people who identify as psychic mediums. Sometimes I received so much information I couldn't make heads or tails about it. It would take time for my mind to process the information I had received. Other times, the information shared in a session would be so spot on, I instantly recognized it as truth. Some of those communications have stayed with me for years.

As I have described earlier, many cultures and traditions hold celebrations of love held for those who have crossed over, welcoming their spirits back home during the time of Samhain, Halloween, Día de los Muertos, or All Saints Day. People have had a reverence for the dead and the desire to communicate with their dearly departed loved ones for as long as we have inhabited this planet. Mementos, clothes, jewelry, and heirlooms belonging to your loved ones take on enormous sentimental value, becoming more precious with each and every year after your loved one has passed. Keeping those precious items can be a true balm

to a grieving soul. What may be an item that brings on waves of grief in the early days of death, may morph into joy. Time can be a healer for a precious object that once produced tears, turning those tears into smiles, as you remember your loved one who has passed, and whose spirit is now on the "other side."

There is a big difference between the Warrens keeping the artifacts they collected in their home, as opposed to keeping them in a separate building. The artifacts the Warrens collected were not loving heirlooms or mementos from beloveds on the other side.

As spiritual, magical people, we know all things carry an essence, and may be imprinted with memories. Dolls can, and do, establish energetic connections to the past, which is one of the many reasons we love them, because we can and do feel a *connection* to them.

I can appreciate the precautions the Warrens took with the artifacts they collected from their work. Lorraine Warren also stated on many occasions that the museum was blessed and prayed over by religious clergy. Prayers and rituals for protection, reverence, and respect for the unseen, for what we know and don't know but are aware of through our senses is good thing. Those tingly feelings we get show up for a reason.

Early on in my studies, I took a class on herbalism. It was the first time I ever met women who identified with the word "Goddess." I loved being in herbalism class and learning about the healing properties of herbs. I love learning new things.

I've always had a green thumb. I love to garden. I enjoy planting and being in relationship with green, growing plant life. One of my latest happy moments as a plant lover and gardener is I've learned I can get an orchid plant to rebloom! I've also had lots of plantings which didn't go the way I had hoped. I don't seem to be able to get roses to grow and I severely underestimated the invasive properties of hops.

In this herbalism class I attended almost two decades ago, I met a mother and daughter who seemed eager to share they were trying to make

connections to "the other side." I didn't know much at the time about hauntings, ghosts, and apparitions, but I've always trusted my intuition, which has been highly developed since I was a child. The word "clairsentient" is a good descriptor of how I perceive the world.

As I listened to the mother and daughter share their story, something just didn't *feel right* to me. After they finished sharing their story, I can clearly recall going to the bathroom and having an eerie, unsettling feeling, that something else was in the bathroom with me.

This was not the first time I had experienced that feeling. I will share I don't see ghosts or spirits with my two eyes, *and I don't want to!* But I *know* when there is a presence in a room or an area. I've also had the same untoward spooky feeling riding in elevators of the old-timey type, the ones made from wrought iron in old buildings.

One particularly scary moment happened to me as I was riding in the dumb-waiter elevator at The Stanley Hotel, which they have now covered up behind a wall. You wouldn't know a dumb-waiter existed in that space if you hadn't been to The Stanley during some of its earlier incarnations. I like to say, "the Stanley keeps re-inventing itself." The Stanley Hotel is located in Estes Park, Colorado, about an hour and a half north of Denver. It's a beautiful, easy drive to go up and come back down in the same day.

On this particular occasion I was visiting The Stanley Hotel on a day trip with co-workers, as part of a thank you for our hard work. During this visit, we were touring the bottom floor of the hotel, and the door to a full-sized dumb-waiter, large enough to hold an adult, opened. I can still see the wrought-iron door in my mind's eye. An employee was entering the dumbwaiter, and I just matter-of-factly asked her if I could get in with her. They must have called for the dumb-waiter from the upper floor. Why I did that, I will never know, especially knowing how I feel about elevators in old buildings.

As soon as she pulled the wrought-iron door closed, and the elevator began to move, I instantly regretted my decision. I felt a horrible intrusive presence in the dumb-waiter. The employee could clearly see the distress on my face.

She asked me, "Do you feel that?"

"Yes," I replied.

She said, "I hate this thing!"

It was a moment I'll never forget. I made her feel validated that she wasn't imagining what she was feeling, and she did the same for me.

Spiritually speaking, we know elevators go between worlds. They are portals within liminal spaces. You push a button, trusting the elevator will go to your desired floor. The doors close, you can't see out, and if all goes well, you'll spend a few moments giving yourself over to not knowing what is really is going on outside those doors, but trusting that, in a very short amount of time, the elevator doors will open, and you will go on your merry way. On subsequent visits to the Stanley, I noticed the dumb-waiter elevator is no longer visible or accessible. It appeared the space in the wall that housed the dumb-waiter had been painted over and covered with plaster. Maybe somebody took the hint! Perhaps the next time we stop in at the Stanley, I'll be courageous and ask about the elevator.

Of course, not all elevators are creepy, and you may never experience what happened to me. I can use a modern elevator with no problems. Modern elevators are also equipped with call buttons and a telephone receiver to call for help. Push a button or pick up the phone and our dear first responders will come to your assistance. But I stay clear of old wrought-iron elevators and dumb-waiters.

To return to our story about the mother and daughter team who wanted to have contact with the other side, as I exited the bathroom on that day, I clearly felt that something was hovering around me. The class was nearing the end, and it was nighttime as we left the building. I got into my car and began to drive home, when I heard what sounded like

something being thrown around in my trunk. There are a number of trunk items I routinely carry, such as extra water, a flashlight, park chairs, an emergency roadside kit, and it sounded like they were being thrown around in trunk area. At the time I was driving a Jeep Cherokee, so the trunk area was right behind the back seat. I was freaking out! I looked in my mirror but saw nothing, but clearly things were being thrown around in a spiritual sense. I could *hear it* but when I looked back, nothing had moved! Something was clearly unhappy.

It took me time to gather myself and calm down, as I was driving! I knew I needed to get it together before I and whatever was carrying on in the back had an accident. After I calmed down so I could keep driving, I realized this was a spirit from the mother and daughter team. When I safely arrived home, I lit a sage bundle and a candle and told the spirit to please leave. I also told the spirit I knew they didn't belong here and had been conjured up without permission. It was okay for them to leave.

At my next herbalism class, I forcefully spoke to the mother-daughter team. When I confronted them, they admitted they had been doing work to call up a spirit. I admonished them for dabbling in things in which they were not skilled, and suggested they figure out how to send the spirit back to where she belonged.

I was never bothered by the woman's spirit again.

CHAPTER SEVEN

Personal Stories and Anecdotes

As I have shared my love of dolls and traveled to different places with them, carrying them along with me as a presenter at conferences, I have been blessed to meet people who are eager to share their personal stories and their relationships with dolls.

At these events, I quickly become known as the "doll lady." I love hearing people's stories about their own dolls, whether they're dolls who belonged to their families, dolls who may have gone missing, or dolls they aren't quite sure how to handle.

I seem to be gifted with the ability to tap into these stories and help people with their dolls. I can hear their sincerity and appreciate the feelings they have when they finally meet someone they can talk to about their dolls without being judged as being cuckoo or crazy.

I love being able to assist them and their dolls in forming a happy relationship, or perhaps to help people to realize the doll may need to move on, if warranted. Sometimes people are very sure they know what the doll needs, but after speaking with me, we come to an "a-ha!" moment, and the emotion of relief fills the air.

One such story happened at a conference. Sometimes people will come up to me before or after my lecture and talk to me in hushed tones about their dolls. I am so honored to listen and hear their stories.

A wonderful lady at a conference I attended as a featured presenter sat down at my table as I was preparing for my lecture.

She began to tell me the story of a doll she had purchased for her daughter years ago. Unfortunately, no matter how hard she tried, her daughter wanted nothing to do with the doll. This situation had caused her much anxiety as she had invested a lot of time and effort into procuring a doll she was sure her daughter would love.

I listened intently to her story. After some time had passed and it seemed she had gotten some relief just by sharing her story, I said to her, "It's not your daughter's doll. That's your doll."

The woman was stunned. I actually saw the look of shock on her face. It took her a moment to grasp what I had said.

During her story, she knew exactly where she had left the doll. She could describe in great detail where she had left the doll in her home, what the doll was wearing, and the emotional toll she had weathered trying to get her daughter to "love" the doll.

I sat with her while her emotions welled up as she took in the significance of what I had shared with her.

I helped her realize the doll was attached to *her.* There was nothing sinister, creepy, or eerie about the attachment, it was just the way it was, and her daughter was honoring her own emotions and boundaries by refusing to have anything to with the doll.

I must say, all this information was a bit difficult for the lady to process. I was very excited we had solved her dollie issue, and hoped she would attend my presentation, which I was due to teach later that afternoon.

She declined to attend. She actually steered far away from me each time I saw her or passed her at the conference. Although I was saddened she didn't attend my lecture, I understood what had happened, as that was not the first time I had shaken people by my innate doll knowledge.

It's okay. This is a gift I have, and sometimes even at a metaphysical or spiritual conference, where people attend because of the spiritual, magical nature of the event, my connection to dolls can be a bit unnerving. It's all right. If a doll and I have an instant connection, or I feel a connection to a person's doll story, I honor it. It's okay if that connection isn't for everyone.

I had another wonderful "aha" doll moment at a conference. A woman in attendance was very happy to share with me her love of dolls. Not only did she love dolls, but she also repaired dolls, which is indeed a valuable skill. Many doll hospitals across the country have closed or gone out of existence. It can be very difficult to find someone to repair your doll. I once took one of my elder dolls to a doll hospital for repair. Her head had come unattached from her body. For years I kept her body and her head in a shoebox. When I finally found a doll hospital, I took her in for repair. I was so excited she was going to have her head re-attached. Apparently even though I appreciate Wednesday and Morticia's love of headless dolls in *The Addams Family*, I like my dolls to have their heads.

I left my doll with the doll hospital staff and eagerly waited for them to contact me. When I went to pick her up, they told me they couldn't find her! Somehow, she had gotten misplaced. What?! I had that doll for years. She had spent decades in a shoebox. I always knew where I kept her. Now I had taken her to the doll hospital for repair and they had lost her!

Clearly, I was distressed. The staff assured me they would find my doll. It wasn't too long after that I got a call that my doll had been found and her head had been re-attached. I wasted no time hurrying to the doll hospital to pick her up. I couldn't wait to see her. It had been years since her head had been attached to her body.

I almost burst into tears when I saw her. Not only had they reattached her head, they had given her lovely clothes and shiny shoes to match. My baby! I was excited to bring to her home. The dollie hospital staff had exceeded my expectations. Not only had they found her, but

they had also dressed her in fine clothing. My heart was full. As I eagerly waited to pay my bill, a customer awaiting service approached me about my doll. They wanted to buy her. No way! Furthermore, one of the staff pulled me aside and whispered to me that the person trying to buy my doll was a collector. They told me my doll was a highly valued collectible doll and that I should never sell her to a collector. Who knew?! Of course, my doll is more valuable to me than money, and I would never consider selling her, but it was very nice of the doll hospital to clue me in on her monetary value.

Of course, I brought her home and placed her on my shelf, in her own special area. I love her and I'll always remember someone tried to buy her from me in the doll hospital.

Having had my own experience with repairing a doll, I appreciated learning the woman telling her story to me at the conference was skilled in doll repair. She shared with me that she was having issues with a doll she had recently acquired as an heirloom.

She had re-furbished the doll with new clothing. She had given her a place of honor in her home, but she could sense the doll wasn't comfortable no matter where she seemed to place her. She had pictures of the doll, which she showed me.

"That's not the same doll," I told her.

"What?" she replied in disbelief.

I told her the pictures of the doll she showed me were not the same doll. I could clearly tell the doll was very unhappy in her most recent photo. The woman then showed me a picture of the doll with a little girl who had been the doll's original owner. In that photo the doll looked happy and content.

I looked deeply at the photo. After studying it for a moment, I told her it was the hair. The doll was not happy with her hair. A-ha! She then shared with me when she was re-furbishing the doll she had used a wig she wasn't quite happy with and didn't feel the wig was quite the fit she

was searching for, for her doll. She told me she had planned to replace the wig with a better wig, but time had gotten away from her, and she had yet to give the doll better hair.

"That's it. She hates her hair," I told her.

It was a great moment. It totally resonated with the woman that the doll didn't like her hair. She said she would fix the doll's hair as soon as she got home.

Sharing the Love of Dolls

The author with Jasmine Williams and their dolls.

Every time I look at the photo, I get immense joy. Many thanks to Jasmine Williams for allowing me to include in my book this photo of her and her dolls standing beside me and my dolls.

Jasmine Williams attended my lecture, The Spiritual Magick of Dolls, at the Mystic South Conference, which was held in Atlanta, Georgia in 2023. After the lecture was over, she asked if she could introduce her dolls to my dolls!

I was ecstatic to have her dolls meet my dolls. Jasmine shared with me she had brought her dolls specifically to the conference to meet my dolls. She had carried her dolls, her beautiful Black dolls, all the way to the conference. Wow! It was indeed a moment of recognition (you have been seen!) and joy when we had our photo taken. I loved meeting her dolls. My dolls loved meeting her dolls. I was very touched by our dollie meet and greet!

Representation matters. It was a joyful experience to see her with her Black dolls, and to revel in the magic that passed as we stood in that moment. Jasmine and her dollies knew they were not alone. My dolls make new friends wherever they go. Jasmine was kind enough to post our photo on social media, and also gave me permission to post the photo on my social media and within the pages in this book, so people could see the joy and happiness of our dolls meeting each other, and the new friendship Jasmine and I have formed.

Coincidences? I think not. The old adage holds true: "there are no coincidences." I was thrilled Jasmine brought her dolls to meet me and attend my lecture.

For years I have been a patron of a local store in our neighborhood. When you live in a neighborhood for as long as we have, which at the time of this writing is approximately thirty years, local businesses become friends. (In addition, our house is almost a hundred years old!) They become places and people you enjoy not only for what they provide, but also the camaraderie you've established over the years.

On a clear, breezy October day, I stopped into one of my local neighborhood stores. As fate would have it, the store was practically devoid of customers. The owner, who has always shown an interest in my work as a writer, asked me how I was doing.

I was in a bit of a funk. I had been at my keyboard all morning, and was feeling exasperated trying to get words on the page, which was why I decided I needed a break from writing. I knew if I went shopping in his store, it would give me respite from the page.

Mind you, I have been a customer for years at this business. The owner has purchased my books, which I deeply appreciate as a writer and a customer. However, I have never discussed what I am working on with him. I tend to keep details about my writing hush-hush until my project is finished, and I have submitted my manuscript to my editor. Call it my own superstitions, but that's how I roll. I don't openly discuss my work until I've submitted it.

Somehow, on this day, I found myself whispering to him, "Would you like to know what I'm writing about?" He leaned in. I swore him to secrecy. We did a pinky swear.

"Dolls," I said. "I'm writing about dolls."

It was as if time stood still, and the mystery of the unknown paused and took a breath. I could see and feel a recognition in his eyes.

He took out his phone. He asked if he could show me a photo.

"Of course."

And there on his phone was a photo of little porcelain doll who obviously some would put in the "haunted" category.

I couldn't believe it. I have been a customer of his business for years, and we have never discussed dolls. Not once. Not ever.

I was giddy. I started laughing.

"She's beautiful!"

He proceeded to show me not one photo but many photos of dolls he has in his collection. We talked at length about our love of dolls, collecting them, mysterious things about the occult, and other "spooky" things.

By this time, the store began to fill with customers. I decided I should let him attend to his other customers, as we could talk about dolls all day. I was ecstatic to learn after all these years, as a loyal patron of his business, he is a doll collector. He not only understands the haunted and the spooky, but he also appreciates it. It was validating for both of us to realize we walk similar paths. I was glad I had *listened* to my intuition and shared my latest writing project with him.

He has since shared many photos of his doll collection with me. I'm looking forward to the day I meet his dolls in person!

In May 2023, I was absolutely thrilled to receive an invitation to speak at a conference hosted by the NYU Steinhardt Department of Art and Art Professions and *The Witch Wave Podcast*, located at NYU Steinhardt in October 2023. A lot of good things happen during the month of October. It must be the season and power of witches! I was very pleased that authors and conference organizers Pam Grossman and Jesse Bransford accepted my proposal to teach about my dolls.

I had a blast at the conference. My mind went into overdrive, listening to all the wonderful teachers share their material. I learned a lot, I had fun, my heart was filled with joy that I was able to present my topic, and I made some marvelous new friends. A few months later, when I was back home in Denver, I received an email from Cynthia Conti-Cook. Cynthia had attended my class at the NYU Occult Humanities Conference. She shared with me she had been inspired to write a poem about her dolls and her grandmother after attending my lecture.

Many thanks to Cynthia Conti-Cook for granting me permission to include her correspondence in my book. It appears here in totality, just as I received it:

Dear Najah,

I was so lucky to be present for your inspiring talk about dolls in NYC back in October. It sent me down a path of questions to my mom and grandma about her attic room full of dolls.

I wrote a poem to remember it all, and I wanted to share it with you in gratitude for opening my heart to the love of dolls. The events at the end of the poem started with a text I sent my mom from your presentation!

With love,

Cynthia

My grandmother's dolls

Though I was a tomboy,
quicker to climb into the branches of
my grandmother's apple tree
than cradle a doll,
I remember my grandmother's doll room,
and its magnetic magic.
She and Grandpa raised five children in a small one-story house.
They all shared one bathroom,
the three boys shared a room in the attic.
When there were no more boys living in the attic,
my grandmother carpeted the floor, including the staircase,
with wall-to-wall fluffy pink seventies carpet.
She plastered the walls, floor to ceiling, with pink wallpaper.
When you opened the door downstairs,
standing in the middle of a dark hallway,
pink spilled down the staircase,
and a wave of cheers cascaded
down the steps from tiny dolls.

Dolls sat, squished shoulder to shoulder,
and greeted you from both sides of the stairs
as you ascended.
Their gaze was continuous—extending up the stairs and around
the entire outer edge of the room
in a counterclockwise spiral.
As you walked up and around,
it was impossible not to keep the gaze of the dolls
until you reached a small round table they all seemed to be staring at.
One single chair faced away from the staircase
and towards a small window.
As you sat, dolls surrounded you in a circle,
shoulder to shoulder, always clean and fresh.
On the round table stood a doll
all the plushes, the porcelains and the dolls with painted smiles
seemed to be staring at.
She was taller than them all and is the one I remember best.
A flamenco dancer, she stood strong, with her chest out,
dressed in red with black polka dots and shimmery gold lace.
In college, I studied flamenco dance, and chased it to a summer in Spain.
I learned that flamenco is more than choreography.
Flamenco is the ancient sound, shape, and movement of free people,
and a way of honoring the spirits still protecting them,
through the expression of their shared love and pain.
My grandmother's flamenco doll had the same olive color skin
of my mother's face in the summer.
A black shawl draped on her shoulders extending the frame of her jet-black
hair,
kissed with white roses.
Her dark pupils gazed out of the left corners of her eyes.

Back then, I didn't know what flamenco dance was,
but I knew her beauty was in how she held her head.
Each doll in that room had a world inside of it,
and I spent hours imagining their stories.
I spun tales about who they were, their passions,
and their travels to Grandmother's attic.
It was only recently that I asked my mother,
how did all those dolls come into Grandma's attic?
How did a woman who lived so frugally, cooked from scratch,
and allowed herself few of life's pleasures,
how did Grandma come to have an entire pulsing-pink attic of dolls?
"When my brother Billy was sick at seventeen," my mom said,
"Mom had to stay near the hospital for hours alone,
because Dad had to keep the store open.
She spent that time in antique stores, buying dolls."
Suddenly I saw down her dark eyelids,
staring at armfuls of small dolls
she squeezed close and stifled her cries in.
I saw up the stairs,
after the room had been stripped
of its memories
and smells of the three boys
who lived there, and the one
who never moved out.
I felt her needing
that pink comfort to coax her back upstairs,
the parade crowd on both sides helping her ascend
to a place where she could be with herself, but not alone.
I sat with her surrounded in a room full of love that couldn't leave her.

• • •

I travel to her now as she sits alone in a room with no dolls,
ninety-eight years old in a nursing home.
Her dolls were mostly sold long-ago.

• • •

Recently, in a season when I was rehearsing for a flamenco performance,
I asked my mom, where did that flamenco doll go?
She didn't remember it, let alone recall her whereabouts.
Weeks passed.

• • •

Mom and her cousin came to see me dance. She couldn't stop smiling.
She sits across from me and says
our cousin Cindy felt terrible she couldn't come watch you dance,
but that she had something she wanted me to give you. Her eyes glisten.

It was a doll Grandma had given her when she started teaching Spanish. She had a picture of her standing tall on her desk, next to Mary. The flamenco dancer.

• • •

Thank you, Cynthia, for your heartfelt, inspiring words!

Personal Connections

In February 2023, I took my first voiceover class at the Denver Center for Performing Arts. As I am a frequent guest on podcasts and a lecturer at conferences and workshops, I believed taking a class would help me in my career. I was also hopeful education and training would lead to work as a narrator.

My voiceover class at the Denver Center for Performing Arts was life-changing. I met so many dedicated people who wanted a career in the arts. I made networking connections that unlocked many doors. Just breathing the air in the Robert and Judi Newman Center for Education

was like oxygen to my blood. As of this writing, I've yet to be cast as a narrator or voiceover actor, but I am just getting started. I have been cast in other projects I would have never thought would be open or be available to me. But when you actively take steps in the direction of your dreams, the Universe will open doors you may have never considered, and those open doors can turn out to be better than the doors you were convinced were in your best interest!

I have been in love with movies, television and films since I was a child. I imagine you may have come to realize this as you read my chapter Hollywood Dolls.

As I spent my formative childhood years in Los Angeles, seeing actors in a local restaurant or film crews setting up on location was part of daily life. It's something you accepted about living in LA, but you also tried to remain cool if you did happen upon an actor, or a movie or TV show being filmed.

As a child, my family home was not far from Hollywood. I have fond memories of going to the Hollywood and Vine area, walking around, hanging out at Grauman's Chinese Theatre, as it was called back then, having lunch or dinner and seeing a celebrity, or looking at the handprints in the Hollywood Walk of Fame. I was imprinted with the love of movies and the magic of Hollywood at a very young age.

Growing up in Los Angeles, the city of dreams, magic, and Hollywood, brings me back to taking my first voiceover class at the Denver Center for Performing Arts and my love of dolls.

You can hold onto a dream so long and hard that it literally hurts. In a moment of introspection and reflection, I realized how much I had always wanted to be in a movie, a film, or have some type of role, no matter how small in the movies. It's easy to see how and why I had that desire, now that I've shared some of my backstory.

I also realized during this time of introspection and reflection that some of my happiest times were attending a Broadway show or going

to the movies. As a writer, my imagination is key. Broadway shows and movies are my happy places. They provided an escape from the mundane world, a place to relax and allow storytellers and actors to take you on adventures that for a few hours only exist in your mind. When I realized how much joy seeing a Broadway show or watching a movie brings me, I decided it was time to take action and enroll in a class at the DCPA.

I had no idea my voiceover class would lead me to actual movie projects and being cast in films and creating a professional portfolio. I'm grateful for all the roles and projects I've been cast in thus far. Each new project is a learning opportunity. I've met great people who also share my same passion for the industry. As of this writing, I've also enrolled in an acting class, titled Acting for the Camera, at DCPA. I'm already learning so many new ways to polish and hone my skills as an actor!

In 2023, during a shoot for a spec commercial, I made fast friends with a working actor who has been in the industry for several decades. One of my first lessons I learned in the industry is that when you are on set you do a lot of sitting around and waiting to be called, resulting in fast bonding with everyone who is also on set that day. You become fast friends for several hours or days, depending upon how many scenes you have been cast in as an actor. You may never see those people again after the shoot is over, but for those several hours you are on set, you share lots of stories. It is a wonderful way to pass the time while you are waiting to be called for your scene.

On this particular day, as we were waiting to be called, the conversation turned to the art of writing and topics I find interesting. Somehow, we ended up discussing dolls!

In a candid moment, my new-found buddy shared with me that, at one point during his career, to make some money on the side (we know actors wear a lot of hats), he owned a company that provided clean-up for estates after someone has died. A lot of people pass away with no one to care for or dispose of their estate. Sad but true.

His company provided services to enter a home, inventory the belongings, and contact next-of-kin, if possible, as to their wishes regarding properties found. If no contact was available, everything went into a dumpster or to an agency such as Goodwill.

He shared with me that during once such service they entered a home to begin their inventory. As they made their way through the home of the deceased, downstairs into the basement, they came upon tens of dolls hanging from the ceiling! He was so stunned by the discovery that he took a photo, which he showed to me on his phone.

Neither he nor his staff had any idea why the deceased had dolls hanging from the basement ceiling. The dolls were clearly out of view of anyone who would enter the house, unless you entered the basement, but nonetheless there they were: dolls suspended from the ceiling!

Just like magic, dolls are everywhere!

During the 2023 NYU Occult Humanities Conference, when I wasn't teaching, I sat in the audience to listen to all the other teachers. Every presenter was a leader in their field, and listening to their presentations was akin to taking a master class in the arts. As I was sitting in my chair during a break, a dear woman asked me if I would be attending the conference the next day. She told me she had something for me. I told her I would be there the next day, and I looked forward to seeing her.

The next day she arrived with a beautifully wrapped box. Inside the box was a doll that had sat on her shelf for thirty years. She told me it was time for her to start clearing out her apartment and she knew her doll would have a good home with me. I was incredibly touched and at a loss for words. I took her doll back to my hotel and introduced her to my dolls. She now lives on a shelf, in her own space with the rest of my dolls and magical things. It is an honor to have her as part of my family.

My Own Personal Story: Working with My Dollies

The three dollies in my collection, whom I have introduced to you through the words on these pages, are magickal. They travel with me, live in my office, share desk space with me, and provide inspiration and comfort to me. We are a magickal family.

During the writing of this book, I had to face a fear. Our home was built in 1929. It is almost a hundred years old. It is one of the good ones. It is a brick bungalow, Craftsman style home. We love its character, style, and all the bricks that make for a solid foundation. But one thing we've learned after living in our home for almost thirty years is that old homes, especially those made of brick, can have their own unique share of maintenance problems.

As I was writing this book, committing words to the page, the city of Denver undertook a massive water project. Denver Water and their fabulous, amazing crew took to our neighborhoods to replace old pipes that had been confirmed to be made of lead. It was a major undertaking. It required turning off our water for hours, not being able to park on our streets, and the sound of heavy equipment, and lots of maintenance workers on the street for hours and days at time. In the end, Denver Water did their job, and I thank them for their amazing work. The crews were exceptionally conscientious about our homes and properties.

During the spring of 2024, I had completed my own massive landscaping project. Using only a shovel and a wheelbarrow, I laid by hand, all by myself, three and a half tons of pink rock on our curbside area, which is also called the "hell strip," because nothing grows there, and it is also super hard to maintain. After years of back-breaking work to keep the area clean and free of weeds and debris, I had embarked upon this massive project to upgrade our curbside. Even my neighbors stopped by to tell me how impressed they were with my work. As you

can imagine, I was very pleased the workmen returned my pink rocks to their original state. You can't even tell they moved massive areas of land!

But with the construction, and perhaps the time of year and the thankfully cooler days and nights after the long too-too hot summer, and maybe because our home is old, a mouse made its appearance. *Ugh.* I can't stand mice in the house, especially when they run across the floor at night. Outside is their domain. Inside, it's my domain. I consider them a violation when and if I see one in my home. It also sucks that I tend to see them first, because I, along with our faithful dog, am normally the only one up at night, when they are most active.

It had been years since a mouse made its appearance in our house. Actually, now that I'm writing these words, the last time we had an intruder (as I call them), *was* when a neighbor's home was under construction. Thankfully that year hubby laid down traps and also my dear service provider came and helped seal up the outside of our home. No more mice.

But this interloper was different. It first scurried across the floor one late night as I was watching TV. Immediately, when I got up the next day, I went to the hardware store and got traps and pet safe repellent. I also called my service provider, and they came the following day. I didn't see the mouse again, and I felt comforted we had done our best to send it on its way.

But after a couple of weeks passed, while checking the traps for a capture, I noticed the peanut butter was gone, but there was no mouse in the trap. I had always depended on hubby or the service to set the traps. But now I realized I needed to step up, face my fears, summon up my courage, learn how to set a trap, and place them in hopes of catching the mouse. So that's what I did. I set new traps and was hopeful that that would be the end of the story. I didn't see any further "activity."

And then the intruder ran across the floor late one night when I was up alone, watching TV.

I was pissed.

Normally I become catatonic when I see one, but now I felt we were at war! That rodent had been eating all the peanut butter and avoiding the traps. What the hell! The thing was testing me!

After I laid more traps, I banged on the floor and stomped around. I wanted to make sure the rodent knew I was serious about catching it. And then I looked at my dollies. I looked deeply into their eyes, and I asked them to please help catch the mouse and that it be dead!

Shortly after I went to bed, I was pretty sure I heard the snap of a trap. When I got up in the morning, I found it in one of my traps! *I had caught it*!

Now perhaps if you live in rural area, or aren't squeamish about mice running across your floor, this story will not be a big deal to you. But it was a *big deal* for me. I had never set a mouse trap. I'm okay with checking them after they set them, but I had never set one on my own. When that mouse ran across the floor when I was alone, after all that had been done to catch it, that was the line. It was time to defend my territory. Words do not do justice to the elation and rush I felt when I found that sucker in the trap, dead.

After I confirmed the dead body, I looked at my dollies and said, "Thank you." Because I have developed a relationship with my magickal dolls, when I needed an ally to help me shore up my strength, to rid my home of the mouse intruder, I went to them. I share this story so you can see how building a relationship with your dolls on a magickal level, if you decide that is something you wish to do, can help you in your time need.

My dollies were happy to assist me! I asked *them* to help catch the mouse, empowering them to do what they do, on their own. And they did.

A Rare Find

As I brought the pages of this book to a close, the Toy and Doll Super Show rolled into Denver. I had never been to a show like this before, and I was excited to go and see all the dolls, as well as pass out the fabulous promo cards my publisher had designed for this book.

Hubby, in his true spirit of support, was excited to join me. At our age we don't get out as much as we used to, so we are happy when an opportunity presents itself to get out and be with the people.

Going to a collector's show on a Sunday afternoon is right up our alley.

We drove to the event venue, which wasn't far from our home, found parking, and made the walk to the event building. A plus! We had made it!

As soon as we entered the exhibit hall, the excitement and good energy was palpable. There were rows of tables and vendors selling dolls, toys, old electronics, and guitars. We set our sights on heading to the aisles filled with dolls.

Oh, my heart! So many dolls! Dolls of all shapes, sizes, ages—some in original boxes, some displayed in rocking chairs, some piled together in big heaps. It was great! Immediately we started down an aisle, allowing ourselves to be led by our intuition and the dazzling arrangement of dollies.

It didn't take long for me to arrive at a table filled with interesting dolls. I quickly found myself in a friendly conversation with the vendor. She was a jovial woman and, to add to our camaraderie, I learned she was from the local Denver area. A win-win! I handed her my promo card. She was interested in my book, and as we talked, I came upon a doll lying naked on her table.

Poor thing! She was completely naked and bald! Her head had sticky patches where her wig must have been attached but had since long disappeared.

1930's Arranbee vintage R&B doll, with new hair.

I immediately picked her up. She had a red tag attached to her arm that read: "Vintage R&B (Arren bee) $10.00."

Hm. I knew she was special.

The vendor and her co-vendor began telling me they believed this doll was made in the 1950s. Besides the tag on her arm, they didn't know much more about her history.

I knew she was coming home with me. The way she was lying naked on her back on the display table with her bald head exposed, clutched at my heart. Instant decision. I purchased her. The vendors lovingly wrapped her up in a diaper to protect her fragile head. I put her in my bag, and we continued strolling, sauntering down the aisles of the Super Show.

Arranbee, found on the full moon, now fully restored and welcomed to the family by dollie number three. This is true doll magic!

Earlier in this book, I gave detailed instructions on how to bring your "new" doll home, and integrate them into your life. I did just that. I followed my own routines for bringing a dollie into our family.

However, I did look up my new dollie in my doll research encyclopedias, and I found her!

The correct spelling is "Arranbee." I found photos in the encyclopedias, as well as online, of similar dolls. She is from the 1930s, which makes her approximately ninety-five years old. She is also worth a lot more than ten dollars. Wow!

After she sat and rested for a while, I began to try and dress her. She needed a covering. As a doll lover, as well as a witchy, magical, spiritual, crafty, and creative person, I have lots of fabrics and things I hold onto, knowing they might have a purpose at a later date.

Recently, as I was picking through some of my craft things, I came across a wig that belonged to one of my dolls long ago. I'm not sure how the wig came off one of my doll's head, but I kept it. When I came across the wig again, instead of putting it back in the drawer where I keep my crafty things, I left it on the counter, which we found hilarious. You have to appreciate what life is like living in my witchy, spiritual, imaginative home.

I knew now why I had left the wig on the counter. It was waiting for a new dollie. I wasted no time in trying it on my "new" Arranbee doll, and it fit her perfectly! She loved it. It looks great on her.

She is no longer naked. She's been dressed, blessed, and accepted into our family. One of my dollies is already especially sweet on her.

A doll's story is never ending.

In Conclusion

It is my sincere desire that the words I have written will be a help and guide unto you as you work with dolls, especially dolls you may feel are of a magical nature.

If you love dolls, may this book help you find ways to be even closer to them. If you've been curious about dolls or are perhaps slightly afraid of them, may this book help alleviate some of those fears. May it give you tangible ways to connect and have loving relationships with dolls, if that is your desire.

If you have dolls or know of dolls that may benefit from being re-homed, may these words also be a comfort and a guide unto you.

It should be noted I also have a collection of Black dolls who simply grace my home with their beautiful presence. I love looking at them and talking to them. They touch my heart. I am sure one day they will all increase in value as creations that magnify and represent the beauty of Black women and little Black girls.

If you happen to see me at a conference or workshop, please feel free to speak to me about your dolls or bring them to meet me. You can also follow me on Instagram and Facebook. I love seeing photos of people with their dolls.

I wish you joy in your doll journeys! May you and your dollies be blessed!

Blessings,
Najah Lightfoot

Bibliography

Coleman, Dorothy S., Elizabeth A., and Evelyn J. *The Collector's Encyclopedia of Dolls,* vol. 2. New York, NY: Crown Publishers, 1986.

Cunningham, Scott. *Cunningham's Encyclopedia of Magical Herbs.* St. Paul, MN: Llewellyn Publications. 1998.

Hundley, Jessica, and Pam Grossman. *Witchcraft.* Köln, Germany: Taschen, 2021

Lightfoot, Najah. "Magickal, Mystical Salt." *Llewellyn's 2015 Magical Almanac: Practical Magic for Everyday Living.* Woodbury, MN: Llewellyn Publications, 2014.

———. *Powerful Juju: Goddesses, Music & Magic for Comfort, Guidance & Protection.* Woodbury, MN: Llewellyn Publications, 2022.

Merrill, Madeline Osborne. *The Art of Dolls 1700–1940.* Cumberland, MD: Hobby House Press, 1985.

Octopus Books. *Encyclopedia of Magic and Superstition.* London, England: Phoebus Publishing Company, 1974.

Sauer, Julia L. *Fog Magic.* U.S.A. Scholastic Book Services, 1970.

Yronwode, Catherine. *Hoodoo Herb and Root Magic: A Materia Magica of African-American Conjure and Traditional Formulary Giving the Spiritual Uses of Natural Herbs, Roots, Minerals, and Zoological Curios.* Forestville, CA: Lucky Mojo Curio Company, 2022.

Ziegler, Gerd. *Tarot—Mirror of the Soul: A Handbook for the Thoth Tarot.* Newburyport, MA: Weiser Books, 2023.

Photo Credits

Page viii. Oldest documented doll. Adapted from photo © IIMK RAS/ *The Siberian Times*

Page ix. Venus of Willendorf. Bjørn Christian Tørrissen, CC BY-SA 4.0, via Wikimedia Commons

Page xi. Matryoshka dolls. Photo by Arthit Pornpikanet/*iStock.com*

Page 13. Photo from the author's collection.

Page 19. Photo by Philip Cacka/*iStock.com*

Page 20. Photo by sqback/*iStock.com*

Page 28. Photos by Alex Black/*iStock.com*

Page 32. Photo by Philip Cacka/*iStock.com*

Page 33. Seminole dolls, Big Cypress, Florida, circa. 1895-1905. In the collection of the National Museum of the American Indian, Smithsonian Institution, Washington, D.C.

Page 35. Photo from the author's collection.

Page 38. Photo from the author's collection.

Page 40. Photos from the author's collection.

Page 44. Photo by Anthony Camera.

Page 50. Photo by Anthony Camera.

Page 54. Photo by Anthony Camera.

Page 56. Photo by Mario Krpan/*iStock.com*

Page 60. Photo by Joe Potato/*iStock.com*

Page 62. Photo from the author's collection.

Page 65. Photo from the author's collection.

Page 86. The Addams Family 1965, Collection Christophel/Alamy Stock Photo

Page 108. Prop Annabelle doll. Photo © Tinseltown/*Shutterstock.com*

Page 129. Clay dolls. Left: photo by FSTOPLIGHT/*iStock.com* right: photo by Dmitry Sosulin/*Dreamstime*

Page 140. The dolls of Isla de las Muñecas. Esparta Palma, CC BY 2.0, via Wikimedia Commons

Page 142. Isla de las Muñecas. Photo by Miguel Rodriguez Silva (MRS)/ *iStock.com*

Page 161. The author with Jasmine Williams. Photo from the author's collection.

Pages 176–177. Arranbee. Photos from the author's collection.

Page 184. Photo of the author by Anthony Camera.

About the Author

Najah Lightfoot is the award-winning author of *Powerful Juju* and *Good Juju*. A prolific writer, she has contributed to many publications including Taschen's *Witchcraft: The Library of Esoterica*, vol. 3. Najah's magickal staff is a part of the permanent collection of the Buckland Museum of Witchcraft and Magick in Cleveland, Ohio. Najah is an in-demand speaker for conferences, events, and workshops. She lives in Denver, Colorado, where the blue skies and the power of the Rocky Mountains uplift and fill her soul. She can be found online at *craftandconjure.com*.

To Our Readers

Weiser Books, an imprint of Red Wheel/Weiser, publishes books across the entire spectrum of occult, esoteric, speculative, and New Age subjects. Our mission is to publish quality books that will make a difference in people's lives without advocating any one particular path or field of study. We value the integrity, originality, and depth of knowledge of our authors.

Our readers are our most important resource, and we appreciate your input, suggestions, and ideas about what you would like to see published.

Visit our website at *www.redwheelweiser.com*, where you can learn about our upcoming books and free downloads, and also find links to sign up for our newsletter and exclusive offers.

You can also contact us at *info@rwwbooks.com* or at

Red Wheel/Weiser, LLC
65 Parker Street, Suite 7
Newburyport, MA 01950